QUITE LITERALLY

QUITE LITERALLY

Problem Words and
How to Use Them

Wynford Hicks

Routledge
Taylor & Francis Group

LONDON AND NEW YORK

First published 2004
by Routledge
11 New Fetter Lane, London EC4P 4EE

Simultaneously published in the USA and Canada
by Routledge
29 West 35th Street, New York, NY 10001

Routledge is an imprint of the Taylor & Francis Group

© 2004 Wynford Hicks

Typeset in Bembo by Taylor & Francis Books Ltd
Printed and bound in Great Britain by
TJ International Ltd, Padstow, Cornwall

British Library Cataloguing in Publication Data
A catalogue record for this book is available from the British Library

Library of Congress Cataloging in Publication Data
Hicks, Wynford, 1942–
Problem words / Wynford Hicks.
p. cm.
Includes bibliographical references.
1. English language—Usage—Dictionaries. 2. English language—Terms and phrases.
I. Title.
PE1464.H53 2004
423'.1—dc22   2003026061

ISBN 0–415–32019–4 (hbk)

CONTENTS

Introduction   vi
Acknowledgements   xiv

Problem words A–Z   1

Further reading   250

INTRODUCTION

What's an alibi, a bete noire, a celibate, a dilemma? Should underway be two words? Is the word meretricious worth using at all? How do you spell realise – with an s or a z – and should bete be bête? Should you split infinitives, end sentences with prepositions, start them with conjunctions? What about four-letter words, euphemisms, foreign words, Americanisms, clichés, slang, jargon? And does the Queen speak the Queen's English?

This book tries to answer questions like these. It's intended for readers and writers, professional and amateur, established and aspiring, formal trainees and those trying to break in; students of English, both language and literature, and their teachers.

It concentrates on writing rather than speech. It certainly doesn't offer advice on how to pronounce words – there's nothing here about spoken accents. On the other hand, the advice given on how to use words in writing can usually be applied to formal speech – what is carefully considered, broadcast, presented, scripted or prepared for delivery to a public audience – as opposed to informal, colloquial speech.

The book is intended to be practical – and also fun. Many of the points made are illustrated with quotes. These come mainly from newspapers, magazines and books – in other words from sources that are publicly available. Although the emphasis is on British usage, papers like the *New York Times* and the *Australian* are included with the *Times* and the *Guardian*.

Some of the quotes are from language experts. This is not an attempt to embarrass them. It is because I have consulted books about language – dictionaries, style and usage books and those written by academic linguists – for their content and in passing found useful examples of usage. See page 250 for a list of books referred to.

It's noticeable that there is something of a divide among those who write about language between the conservatives and the radicals. The conservatives are committed to standard English;

want to preserve the grammar they were taught at school and extend it to everybody else;

fight to keep the traditional meaning of words and expressions;

think that dictionaries should be prescriptive rather than descriptive.

The radicals, on the other hand,

want to undermine standard English, dismissing it as a mere dialect;

insist that the grammar of 'uneducated' people is just as good as taught grammar;

emphasise that words continually change their meanings – they generally prefer the newer, more popular ones;

think that dictionaries should be descriptive rather than prescriptive.

In their extreme form both these positions are ridiculous and unhelpful. They make the problem of problem words worse.

Take these traditional precepts of old-fashioned English teaching:

don't start a sentence with a conjunction;

don't end a sentence with a preposition;

don't split an infinitive.

These instructions derive from the grammar of Latin, which was used as the model by the first English grammarians. None of them apply to modern English. Splitting infinitives and putting prepositions at the end of a sentence and conjunctions at the beginning are now clearly matters of style not grammar.

(And, by the way, to follow none by a plural instead of a singular verb – as I did in the previous paragraph – isn't a grammatical mistake, either. The belief that it is a mistake is based on the mistaken idea that none always means not one.)

The linguistic conservatives also have a simplistic approach to the meaning of words. To aggravate can only mean to make worse, they say (because it derives from the Latin word *gravis*, heavy); or celibate must mean unmarried (because that is what it used to mean); or fulsome cannot be used in the positive sense of abundant (because in the past it meant excessive).

The linguistic radicals are also inclined to oversimplify in their approach to changing meanings. They tend to see the new ones as driving out the old. Unfortunately, in the case of words like aggravate, disinterested and fulsome, it looks as though both old and new meanings are in current use with neither likely to 'drive out' the other.

Some words have been disputed for centuries – without any signs of a resolution of the dispute. The *Oxford English Dictionary* gives the earliest use (1662) of disinterested as 'without interest' and the earliest use of uninterested (1646) as 'impartial, unbiased'. These definitions are the opposite of the traditional ones.

The case of fulsome is even more striking. According to Kate Burridge, its earliest recorded sense, from the thirteenth century, was 'abundant, full, good'. Gradually the negative senses 'over-abundant, excessive' became dominant. Now, once again, the word is most often used in a positive sense – though this usage is challenged by the conservatives. James Cochrane, for example, says: 'The older meaning should be preserved, if only because it cannot so easily be replaced.'

But disagreements about what individual words mean are superficial compared with attitudes to grammar. The linguistic radicals propose nothing less than the rejection of traditional grammar as the cornerstone of standard English.

They say that standard English is only one dialect among many. A typical view is Kate Burridge's: 'On purely linguistic grounds ... all dialects are equal. All have the same potential, at least, for complexity and richness of expression.'

They say that standard English came about by accident – and at the same time was imposed from above. A typical view is Ronald Wardhaugh's:

> The variety of English that we now refer to as standard English achieved its position by accident. It was the variety of the language that a powerful group in society used at a time when it was desirable to promote that variety in order to consolidate power.

And they say that traditional English grammar should not be preferred to colloquial usage.

Crucial to their argument is a claim about the relationship between speech and writing. They say that languages are originally spoken phenomena and that writing evolved as a way of giving some kind of permanence to speech, which remains primary. Since speech comes first chronologically and logically, its naturally evolving patterns should not be subject to arbitrary rules imposed by grammarians.

In support of their argument the radicals point to the richness that can be found in colloquial and dialect speech. And they make the telling point that to remove the privileged status of standard English would be egalitarian and democratic. Millions of people would no longer suffer from the disadvantage of being told they use language in an inferior and ungrammatical way. They would no longer have to labour to acquire standard English in order to write acceptably.

This argument is attractive, particularly to those who want to promote social equality. But it suffers from several flaws.

First, it is based on a distinction between speech and writing that is crude and simplistic. Speech and writing are not two separate categories, one natural and informal, the other artificial and formal. Speech can be prepared and structured – and in the public world it usually is. Think of barristers and debaters; lecturers and store demonstrators; salespeople with their carefully contrived, rehearsed patter, after-dinner speakers, priests in the pulpit ...

Not everybody is a public speaker but most people from time to time do stop and think before they speak, and so are likely to express themselves in a coherent and structured way. They are more likely on these occasions to try to speak in standard English.

At the same time writing doesn't have to be formal. Hand-written personal letters have often been rushed onto the page, punctuated by a series of dashes rather than full stops, written in snatches rather than complete sentences. Now, thanks to email and text messaging, millions of words are written every day in a loose, unstructured conversational form. Clearly they undermine the rigid speech–writing division.

Speech and writing interact constantly. Broadcast journalists, playwrights and screenwriters obviously need to keep the immediacy and freshness of speech. But successful print journalists and novelists write with their ears, too. The spoken word – above all when used in broadcasting – has a huge influence on the written word. Sentences are shorter nowadays; there's more elision (there is becoming there's); and in general grammar is simpler and looser. It would be difficult now – except in parody – to write: 'For whom tolls the bell?'

So rather than a speech–writing division, it makes better sense to distinguish between the informal, personal, colloquial style we use in both speech and writing to communicate with people like ourselves, friends, family, members of the same group, club, tribe – which is geared to them and not necessarily in standard English – and our public voice. This has to be in standard English if we want to ensure that we are understood.

For the second flaw in the radicals' position is that their historical claims are irrelevant. However standard English came about, it is now our public language. It has to be learnt by anyone who wants to take part in the public world of politics, media and culture, as a writer or speaker. This point is – reluctantly – conceded by most of the radicals. Ronald Wardhaugh says that standard English 'is probably a necessary ideal for such domains as administration, law, education, and literature'. And Steven Pinker says: 'People should be given every encouragement and opportunity to learn the dialect that has become the standard one in their society and to employ it in any formal settings.'

Since it is our public language it makes sense to accept it as a whole while trying to correct its defects. But unfortunately that is not what the radicals do. Instead they continue to attack its fundamental positions.

There isn't the space to cover in detail all the grammatical points they make. But one stands out as an example of their perversity: the double negative.

Their argument goes like this. In early English a second or third negative word reinforced the first, as in the following quotation from Chaucer:

> He nevere yet no vileyne ne sayde
> In al his lyf unto no maner wight.

In today's colloquial English (Bethnal Green, Brixton, the Bronx) the doubling of the negative has the same force, as in 'I didn't see nothing' (meaning 'I saw nothing').

As well as Chaucer the radicals routinely quote Mick Jagger, who sang: 'I can't get no satisfaction.' And of course there is no ambiguity here – in context the second negative reinforces the first. But around the same time Tom Jones sang: 'It's not unusual', using the second negative to counter the first – that was clear as well.

In standard English 'I didn't see nothing' becomes 'I didn't see anything.' If the word 'nothing' is used instead, the sentence means roughly the opposite.

The fact is that the use of a double negative to assert a positive is not some weird academic throwback: it is a part of everyday English, particularly in its written form. And the evidence for this comes from the writings of the radicals themselves. For however much they claim to disapprove of standard English, they write in it rather than in scouse or cockney.

Steven Pinker, for example, who quotes Mick Jagger with approval, says on page 376 of *The Language Instinct*: 'In the grammar of standard English a double negative does *not* assert the corresponding affirmative.'

But in fact Pinker writes in standard English and uses the double negative. The first words of his book are: 'I have never met a person who is not interested in language.' And his second chapter begins: 'By the 1920s it was thought that no corner of the earth fit for human habitation had remained unexplored. New Guinea, the world's second largest island, was no exception.' How many negatives in that?

As well as the double negative this book focuses on disputed grammatical points like may/can/might, lay/lie, who/whom, due/owing, that/which, will/shall, less/fewer – and like. Some people condemn the use of like to mean such as, as in the previous sentence and in:

Language experts like Robert Burchfield accept this use of like.

Here I agree with Burchfield, whose edition of Fowler is, in my opinion, the best reference book on English usage. But I disagree with his defence of less applied to people, as in:

Less people were there.

Many of these contentious grammatical points are difficult – perhaps impossible – to resolve. My intention in this book is to provide practical advice, but nobody can claim to have written the last word on any of them.

Meaning is the other main focus of the book. With fulsome (excessive or abundant) go words like aggravate (make worse or annoy), celibate (unmarried or abstaining from sex), dilemma (problem or awkward choice between two unwelcome possibilities). Often the choice is between a precise 'educated' meaning and a loose colloquial one – though as the example of fulsome shows, the issue can be more complicated than that. In all these cases the key issue is: what does the word mean to the people using it?

So too with pairs of words with the same root: disinterested/uninterested; sensuous/sensual; masterly/masterful; admission/admittance; and with one triple: assure, ensure, insure. Distinctions between these words are acknowledged by some people but not by all.

Then there are pairs of words that are confused partly because they sound similar in some way, particularly their initial sound: flaunt (display ostentatiously) is confused with flout (treat with contempt); militate (contend) with mitigate (soften); and prevaricate (evade the truth) with procrastinate (defer action). The more latinate and pretentious the word, the more it qualifies to be called a malapropism, after Mrs Malaprop, in Sheridan's play *The Rivals*, who consistently misuses elaborate words.

English has a lot of such elaborate words – meretricious for flashy, otiose for superfluous, rebarbative for repellent – which most readers will have to look up in the dictionary. In the wrong place they can certainly appear formal, pompous, pretentious. Here in this book they are often labelled 'literary' in an attempt to identify them without implying that they should never be used.

But some 'literary' words are ambiguous: peruse can mean read carefully and just read; quaff can mean drink in large draughts and just drink; reiterate can mean repeat again and again and just repeat. Then there is the word indicate. As well as its unambiguous and straightforward use (of a motorist, signal the intention to turn left or right), indicate can mean point out, show, imply, suggest, state, say.

There is a small but interesting category of paired words that can be called mirror words: imply/infer; learn/teach; ancestor/descendant; lend/borrow. The same action or relationship is described – from two opposite points of view. So if I imply something, you can infer it from what I say. If I teach you something, you learn it. If I am your ancestor, you are my descendant. If I lend you something, you borrow it. Sometimes the wrong one of the pair is chosen. People say: 'Can I lend your book?' Or: 'Please learn me to swim.'

Another word category in the book is homophones and homonyms. A homonym is a word pronounced and spelt the same as another but with an entirely different meaning. So the two words cleave (meaning split) and cleave (meaning join) are homonyms. There aren't many homonyms.

Homophones – two words pronounced in the same way but different in spelling and meaning – are far more common (and the more people rely on computer spell-checking, the more homophone mistakes there will probably be). The *Guardian*'s corrections and clarifications feature is full of homophone mistakes that have appeared in the paper: geyser/geezer; rein/reign; phase/faze ...

On spelling this book makes recommendations within the limits defined by dictionaries. First, it identifies some words commonly misspelt (accidentally not accidently, hiccup not hiccough). Second, it prefers British to American usage (axe not ax). Third, if a word is of foreign origin, the spelling recommended is usually that of the original language (largesse not largess), unless the anglicised spelling is generally accepted (naivety not naïveté). Fourth, spelling distinctions are made if they help to clarify a distinction between two words (linage, payment by the line, as opposed to lineage, descent).

A practice that is not recommended is to use two different spellings of the same word to refer to different types of activity, eg inquiry (for a formal investigation), enquiry (for a simple question) and judgment (for a legal decision), judgement (for a simple opinion). However, in the world of computers where American spelling rules, we now have program and disk, whereas elsewhere we keep programme and disc.

Fifth, a spelling can help to show the most common pronunciation of an unfamiliar word (adrenalin, with a short i, not adrenaline; swathe, with a long a, not swath).

And finally, all other things being equal, the shorter, plainer spelling is preferred to the longer, more elaborate one. So the consonant is not doubled (biased not biassed); or the e is left out (judgment not judgement). The extra syllable is left out (preventive not preventative; dissociate not disassociate) and so is the extra flourish, added by those wishing to create a literary effect (among not amongst; while not whilst).

Examples are also given of words now joined up as one: commonsense as a noun as well as an adjective; underway; onto (as in 'the cat jumped onto the chair' as opposed to 'they went on to London'). Hyphenation is covered and so are various points of punctuation, such as the use of the apostrophe.

There are entries in the book for things like four-letter words, euphemism and jargon; Americanisms, clichés and foreign words; rhyming slang, feminine forms and French. I have also included a number of medical problem words, such as acute, remission and resuscitation, because they are increasingly used by non-medical people.

Finally, my answer to the question 'Does the Queen speak the Queen's English?' comes in the entry on that and which (see pages 226–8).

ACKNOWLEDGEMENTS

'This is just to say' by William Carlos Williams, from *Collected Poems: 1909–1939,* Volume I, copyright © 1938 by New Directions Publishing Corp. Reprinted by permission of New Directions Publishing Corp. and Carcanet Press, Ltd.

Quotes © *Guardian* and © *Observer* appear courtesy of the newspapers.

I would like to thank Christopher Cudmore for commissioning the book, Rebecca Barden for her many helpful suggestions and the copy editor Liz Jones for tidying up the detail; any remaining mistakes are of course mine – if you spot one, send me an email at the address below. Various people contributed problems or solutions including Mark Whitehead, Humphrey Evans, Rene Wyndham and David Poyser. Special thanks to Neville Goodman, joint author of *Medical Writing,* for his advice on medical problem words, and to Tim Gopsill, editor of the *Journalist,* in which some of the material in this book was first published.

Wynford Hicks
wynford@hicksinfrance.net

A

a/an
an replaces a before a vowel (an owl), unless the vowel is sounded as
a consonant (a use), and before a silent h (an hour). Some writers in
the past insisted on using an before words like hotel, habitual,
historical, horrendous and heroic (partly because some upper-class
people didn't sound the h in speech), but this practice was always
dubious and now seems affected. In the following examples it is
ludicrous:

> This was an habitual exchange.
>
> (Donna Tartt)

> It was an horrendous day for a team that proved itself to be the
> best in the country.
>
> (*Sunday Times*)

If you use a before these words – in speech and writing – you will
sound natural and be correct.

abbreviations
no longer need to be marked by full stops, whether they are
truncations (where only the first part of the word is given, as in prof
for professor or in for inch), contractions (where the first and last
letters are given, as in st for saint and rd for road) or single letters
(BBC, PD James). Some abbreviations are spoken and written as
words starting with a capital letter (Nato, Aids): these are called
acronyms. Abbreviations should not be followed by words they
include so ITN news and PIN number are incorrect.

abortion

is the ordinary word for what doctors call a termination (that is, a pregnancy ended by intervention). Technically, an abortion is the premature expulsion of a fetus however caused.

abrogate

cancel, revoke, is confused with arrogate, claim for yourself.

absorb

but

absorption

accede to

is used to mean agree to (a request) and come to (the throne) but it sounds formal elsewhere:

> for women and minorities to accede to positions of real authority.
>
> (*Guardian*)

accents

whether you should keep the accent on a word of foreign origin depends on all sorts of things including how common it is in English and whether the accent distinguishes it from another word of the same spelling. For example, résumé (summary, cv) needs acute accents to distinguish it from resume, whereas château can get by without its circumflex accent. If you put an accent on a word to show how it is pronounced, you must include any other accents it has, so emigré should be émigré and paté should be pâté.

accessible

not accessable

accidentally

not accidently

accolade

high public praise, is confused with acolyte, faithful follower:

When, for the third time, she mentions the 'accolades' who sought to protect Blair I correct her. 'You mean acolytes, Mo.'

(profile of Mo Mowlam, *Sunday Times*)

accommodate
is often misspelt – remember the two m's.

accrue
come as a natural growth or increment, is confused with acquire, get or gain:

> Schools at the bottom of the heap accrue more of society's downtrodden.
>
> (Ted Wragg, professor of education)

achilles heel/tendon
needs no capital A and no apostrophe.

acknowledgement
not acknowledgment

acolyte *see* accolade

acronyms *see* abbreviations

actor, actress *see* feminine forms

actual, actually
are usually padding words with no function in a sentence ('In actual fact it exists', 'He's here, actually'). But they can be used for emphasis. 'He actually arrived early' suggests astonishment that he came at all.

Like literally, actually can be misused to try to justify a stale metaphor:

> The road to hell is – and in this case, actually was – paved with good intentions.
>
> (*Guardian*)

3

No, it wasn't: good intentions didn't become paving stones. See **rhetorical adverbs**.

actualité

a French word meaning topicality or current events which is misused to mean truth in the phrase 'economical with the actualité', a euphemism for lying. Since the Tory politician Alan Clark used the phrase, as a variation on 'economical with the truth', it has become a nonsensical cliché to be avoided. But Anthony Howard, reviewing Tony Benn's diaries in the *Sunday Times*, managed to make the phrase work by using actualité in something like its original French sense:

> Benn, never one to be economical with the actualité, dictated more reams than have ever appeared.

acute

from the Latin *acutus*, means sharp. Thus an acute shortage is a very bad one; acute indigestion is particularly painful; and an acute observation by someone is keenly perceptive. In the sense of severe, acute is contrasted with chronic, which means lingering, lasting, deep-seated. But the two words are often confused: chronic (which sounds bad) is used to mean severe, as in the phrase 'something chronic'.

There is a further problem. In medical jargon acute does not now mean severe at all. Instead the doctors contrast acute (of a condition arising suddenly) with severe (critical or dangerous). Something can be acute without being severe or severe without being acute – or it can be both. Hence the term given in 2003 to a particularly virulent form of flu: severe acute respiratory syndrome (Sars).

But in ordinary English an acute shortage and a severe shortage continue to mean the same thing.

adaptation

not adaption

adapter, adaptor

an adapter is someone who adapts, eg a novel for the stage, while an adaptor is what you need when your electric plug doesn't match the socket.

addenda

is the plural of addendum.

additionally, in addition, in addition to

are formal alternatives to also, as well as.

address

(issues, problems) is political and management jargon for face, apply yourself to:

> One of our own former spy chiefs, Stella Rimington, has said this war will be impossible to win unless we address the underlying causes of terrorism.
>
> *(Guardian)*

> We're much better off having a plan to address the problem proactively rather than reacting to an incident.
>
> *(Australian)*

In real life people address things like envelopes and golf balls – and then act: they take their letters to the post or hit the ball with their club. What politicians and managers do with an issue once they have addressed it is less clear.

See also: **proactive**.

adherence, adhesion

both these words come from the verb adhere which means both stick (to), in the literal sense, and keep (to). Adhesion and its adjective adhesive refer to sticking; adherence and adherent refer to keeping, belonging. Here the wrong one has been used:

> Our secular adhesion to the principles of peace, tolerance and sharing cannot be shaken by expressions of hate.
>
> (Moroccan newspaper report)

adipose

is literary for obese (abnormally fat).

administer

not administrate

admissible

not admissable

admission, admittance

both words come from admit but they are used differently: admission is used of something admitted or conceded (admission of guilt) and the price of entry (admission £5), while admittance is particularly used of attempts to keep people out (no admittance). Here the writer has used the wrong one:

> Hilda ... attends the Left Book Club only because admittance is free.
>
> (Christopher Hitchens)

adrenalin

not adrenaline

advance (planning)

a case of tautology or saying it twice – you can hardly plan after the event.

adverbs

are a problem for most writers. In many cases they are merely padding: 'He currently owns 50 acres'; 'Researchers have successfully developed'; 'The plans were originally drawn up.' And what about the 'merely' in the previous sentence?

There is a tendency to include an adverb automatically, without thinking, as when the New Labour spin doctor Jo Moore said sorry for trying to bury bad British news on 11 September 2001. Her opening words were: 'I want to again sincerely apologise ...' 'Sincerely' sticks out here: who sets out to apologise insincerely?

Then there are the adverbs designed to rescue an impossible or dubious claim, as in 'White Hart Lane was virtually deserted last night' or 'He is arguably England's best player.' Cutting the adverb won't help here: the problem is in the sentence as a whole.

And there are the clumsy ones made to do an impossible job, as in this obituary:

> Even when lucratively denied television, he kept busy on stage
> and in movies.
>
> *(Guardian)*

He can't have been *lucratively* denied since that would mean he made money out of the denial. The writer is struggling to say the opposite.

Even the best writers sometimes trip themselves up over adverbs, as in this example from the stylish TV critic AA Gill:

> What it is, is telly repertory. And I must say, it's appealing. But
> it's also deeply shallow.

Deeply shallow?

The American virus of putting the adverb before the verb when it belongs after it has spread all over the English-speaking world as in: 'Because Windows was not properly shut down ...' The adverb is often, though not always, more effective after the verb.

The following is not English either:

> I would take more seriously your leader if you had not used so
> much of your magazine explaining what jolly fun porno-
> graphy is.
>
> *(Observer* letter)

See also **split infinitive** (for position of adverb) and **literally**.

adverse
meaning opposed, unfavourable, is confused with averse, disinclined, reluctant.

adviser
not advisor but
advisory

aerodrome, aeroplane, airplane

aeroplane, the traditional British spelling of airplane, now looks quaint, although it is still recommended by most authorities. I think that airplane will eventually replace it; in the short term aircraft removes the problem. By contrast the word aerodrome works for a small airfield used by light aircraft – it's an old-fashioned word for something that has changed very little over the years.

affect, effect

the dictionary distinguishes between affect meaning to assume, pretend to have (he affected a false superiority) and affect meaning to influence (the weather affected icecream sales). They are different words. To complicate matters, to effect means to carry out or accomplish (he effected the sale). As a noun affect (in psychology an emotional state) is rare but effect is very common. It means the result of an action (the effect of the weather was increased sales) and in the plural goods, property (his personal effects).

after

there are two ways of saying that something is the second biggest, longest etc while referring to the first. This is the simplest:

> Mr Aznar is, after Mr Blair, the most important and enthusiastic world leader backing the Washington hawks.
>
> (*Guardian*)

It's also possible to say that something comes second while putting the winner in brackets:

> Vietnam ... the world's second-largest exporter (after Thailand).
>
> (*Economist*)

The brackets are essential. When they are left out the effect is to demote the runner-up to third place:

> Texas is the second-most-populous state after California.
>
> (*Economist*)

In fact Texas is the *most* populous American state after California.

aftermath

technically, the aftermath is a second mowing of grass which springs up after the first mowing in early summer, but the word is commonly used to mean the consequences of a particular event:

> The first such settlement, of which all succeeding ones have been modifications, was in the aftermath of the first world war.

> A 'domino democratisation' ... is not likely in the Middle East in the aftermath of even a successful, low-casualty war in Iraq.
>
> (*Guardian*)

> [on swear words] the 1960s and their aftermath brought matters up to date.
>
> (Kingsley Amis)

ageing

not aging

agenda

is now considered a singular word (although it was originally Latin for 'those things that need to be done'); its plural is agendas. Agenda is French (and also American) for diary:

> I fished a worn crocodile agenda with a doubled rubber band around it out of his jacket pocket.
>
> (Dirk Wittenborn)

agents provocateurs

is the plural of agent provocateur.

aggravate

is used to mean make worse (he aggravated the injury) and also annoy:

> He had pronounced and aggravating views on what the United States was doing for the world.
>
> (Graham Greene)

> She notes that he never intends to provoke which is 'in itself
> an aggravation' ... Aggravation is [Penelope] Lively's forte.
>
> (*Observer* book review)

Use with care since purists disapprove of the second usage.

aggression, aggressiveness
aggression always implies a hostile attitude whereas aggressiveness
suggests being assertive.

agreement
or concord is the grammatical principle that a singular subject is
followed by a singular verb and a singular pronoun, whereas a plural
subject is followed by matching plurals. See **number agreement**.
   In the following example variation should be plural to match their:

> Geographical, social, stylistic and personal variation can be
> teased out, and their interaction explored.
>
> (introduction to *The Chambers Dictionary* 1998 by Jean Aitchison)

aid and abet
is lawyer's jargon for help.

akimbo
has a precise meaning: with hand on hip and elbow out. So legs that
are apart can't be akimbo and nor can arms that are waving about.

à la mode
French for a type of stew (boeuf à la mode); American for served with
icecream (apple pie à la mode).

albeit
is formal for although, even if:

> The Ardagh I meet does now sleep, albeit ... attached all
> night to an oxygen machine.
>
> (*Guardian*)

A level
with cap but no hyphen, for advanced level examination

alga
is the singular of algae.

alibi
from the Latin for elsewhere, has a precise meaning known to all readers of crime thrillers; viewers of police procedurals; detectives, villains and their briefs ... It is a suspect's claim that they were somewhere else at the time the crime was committed; by extension an alibi is also the witness who vouches for them. Because it is so widely used and commonly understood in its original sense, alibi is a weak general excuse for failure.

alliteration
repetition of initial sound, should be avoided in serious contexts as in:

> Seven people died in a horrific house fire in Huddersfield.
>
> (newspaper report)

all right
not alright, which still looks wrong

allusive
alluding, hinting, is confused with elusive, practising elusion, deceptive.

almost
is misused before adverbs like literally and invariably; see **literally**, **invariably** and **rhetorical adverbs**.

Alsatian
for a person from Alsace; alsatian is a popular British term for a German shepherd dog.

alternative
although in Latin *alter* means other (of two), it is a superstition that in English you can have only two alternatives. Since the middle of the

11

nineteenth century, the word has been used to mean a choice between more than two things.

although, though
there is no difference in meaning between these two words when they introduce a phrase or clause, though the shorter form is more informal. Only 'though' can be used as a tag-on as in: 'It's a bit colloquial, though.'

alumnae, alumni
are the plurals of alumna and alumnus, ex-students of a particular school or college.

amateur(ish)
amateur, as opposed to professional, is not derogatory, but amateurish means slipshod.

Americanisms
yesterday's Americanism is today's standard (British) English, as with raise for bring up and truck for lorry. But where there is a risk of confusion, prefer British usage to American (unless you are writing mainly for Americans). Some differences between British and American usage are given in this book, eg see **appeal**. For lists of differences see *The Economist Style Guide* (sixth edition), the *Hutchinson British–American Dictionary* and the American–English/English–American glossary published by Abson Books London.

The problem should not be exaggerated. All over the world English speakers grow up with American as their second language or an alternative dialect; they are rarely baffled by it. For non-English speakers, however, there are pitfalls, as is shown by this *Guardian* letter:

> Lecturing at a foreign university, I had a colleague who was convinced that the American sign Parking-Free Zone meant somewhere drivers could park without paying.

amid
not amidst, but prefer among

amok

not amuck

among

not amongst, which is literary

among, between

something is traditionally divided between two people and among three or more. But Lille lies between, not among, Paris, London and Brussels. And the usage 'divide it between the three of us' is increasingly popular and difficult to object to.

ampersand (&)

use to mean 'and' only in official and company names where the organisation uses it.

analyse

not analyze

ancestor

is confused with descendant:

> They [Gibraltarians] 'want to remain British' (though that's a slightly complex concept in a distant sub-colony largely populated by the ancestors of Italians, Greeks and Maltese).
> (*Guardian*)

See **mirror words**.

and, but

there is no reason why these words should not begin a sentence. The belief, encouraged by some English teachers, that this is a breach of literary etiquette is one of the great mysteries.

and ... which, who, that

to introduce a clause, needs an earlier which, who or that; 'and which' should not follow 'that'. See **that, which**.

annex, annexe
use annex for the verb; annexe for the noun.

answerphone
is the ordinary spelling; Ansaphone is the name of a particular brand. To avoid confusion, use answering machine.

anticipate
is often misused as a pompous variant of expect (we don't anticipate rain). It is also used by careful writers to mean forestall or act in advance or come before:

> On social spending, opinion moved sharply rightwards in the 1970s, anticipating Margaret Thatcher's victory.
>
> (*Guardian*)

Sometimes people use it both ways, undermining the subtle distinction: here's film director David Cronenberg:

> Kafka basically anticipated the whole 20th century ... I just always anticipated being an artist.

anti-semitism *see* Semitic

apostrophes
the apostrophe has three uses: to show that something has been left out (don't for do not); to mark a possessive (lamb's liver); and where necessary, to clarify an unusual plural (mind your p's and q's).

With words ending in s, including proper nouns, the apostrophe comes after the s; then an extra s is added if it is sounded (St Thomas's hospital but for Jesus' sake). It's a mistake to put the apostrophe before the s: to call Tony Parsons' book 'Tony Parson's book'. Expressions like two weeks' notice and in two days' time need the apostrophe; for goodness' sake is better with it.

With words like men, women and children the apostrophe goes before the s, as in children's. With names of places and organisations follow their practice (Harrods, Sainsbury's) unless it is obviously illiterate, so never write womens' (apostrophe in the wrong place) or womens (no apostrophe), even if you find the organisation listed this way in the phone book. Menswear, however, is OK.

John o'Groat's in the far north of Scotland is a curiosity. It was originally John o'Groat's house, hence the second apostrophe, but as the house has been dropped from the placename, the apostrophe has tended to go with it. Reference books are divided on whether to keep/restore it.

The most common apostrophe confusion is its/it's. As a possessive its does not take an apostrophe – and nor do his, hers, theirs, yours etc. But when 'it is' is shortened, it becomes 'it's'.

There is no need to use an apostrophe to mark plurals like the 1970s, MPs or Ps and Qs because they are clearly plurals. But p's and q's needs apostrophes. Even this may change: what was once 'do's and don't's' with three apostrophes is now 'dos and don'ts' with one.

appeal
in Britain you appeal against a ruling or judgment; in the US you appeal it.

appendixes
is the plural of appendix, both in books and in the body. The traditional Latin plural appendices (used only of books) is dying out.

appertain
is sometimes used as a formal variation on belong or refer (this comment appertains to him). Worse, it is confused with obtain, meaning apply or hold good, as here:

if the current law on copyright had appertained at the time.
(*London Review of Books*)

appetizer
is American for first course, starter etc.

appraise, apprise
to appraise is to assess the value of; to apprise is to inform, give notice to:

> Governments ... [will want] ... to be appraised of the
> lessons.
>
> (*Guardian* corrections)

approx(imately)
use about.

apropos
with or without of after it, the word apropos (from the French *à propos*) is used to mean to the point or in reference to. And it is also used to mean the opposite: incidentally, by the way. See **opposite meanings**.

archaisms
eg abed for in bed, anon for soon, aught for anything, should be avoided unless you want to sound medieval.

arguably
is often used instead of possibly/probably: since these words have more precise meanings, it is better to choose one or the other rather than blur the issue with arguably.

around
if around means about (he earns around £30,000 a year), use about.

arrogate *see* abrogate

artefact
not artifact

artist
not artiste

as
there are several common mistakes in the use of as. In a comparison there's a tendency to lose the second as: 'He is as old, if not older, than his sister.' This doesn't work because you can't say 'as old ... than': you have to say 'as old as'. So the sentence becomes: 'He is as old as, if

not older than, his sister.' But this sounds very stilted. The more natural-sounding way of saying and writing this is: 'He is as old as his sister – if not older.'

Sometimes in a comparison the verb is left out, which changes the meaning altogether, as here:

> While many Northern Irish Catholics found the Provisional IRA campaign as odious as their Protestant neighbours, it tapped deep into a tacit vein of support.
>
> (*Guardian*)

The writer wants to say that many Catholics hated the IRA as much as the Protestants did – but as it stands the sentence means that the Catholics hated the IRA as much as they hated the Protestants.

In the following example there is conflict between as much and rather than:

> I am as much responsible for that, as a writer, rather than Roy.
> (footballer Roy Keane's ghostwriter Eamonn Dunphy,
> writing in the *Observer*)

Perhaps this is because Dunphy isn't clear himself whether to share responsibility with Keane or to take it from him.

Another mistake is to introduce the redundant word equally as in: 'He is equally as good as his sister.'

assist
is formal for help.

assure
to give confidence to, is confused with ensure (to make happen) and insure (to arrange insurance).

attaché
needs the accent.

attorney general
no hyphen

attrition

which means wearing down, is used as a formal word for loss:

> both churches are suffering membership attrition.
>
> *(Queensland Courier-Mail)*

auger, augur

an auger is a tool for boring holes; an augur was an ancient Roman soothsayer; hence to augur well/badly is to be an encouraging/ discouraging sign.

au naturel

means plainly cooked not in the nude.

aural, oral

aural (referring to the ear) is confused with oral (referring to the mouth).

Australian English

see the Australian–English/English–Australian glossary published by Abson Books London

autarchy, autarky

the first means absolute power and the second self-sufficiency; the first is more common than the second but the two are confused and neither is necessary – why not use absolute power and self-sufficiency?

authoritative

not authoritive

avant la lettre

means before the word or definition was invented (Mary Shelley was a feminist avant la lettre).

aver

is literary for say:

'I realise it could be all over fast,' she avers.

(*Independent on Sunday*)

avoirdupois
the system of weights in which a pound equals 16 ounces is misused in facetious references to excessively fat people, as in this remark by one of Ruth Rendell's characters to another spotted in a supermarket:

'Stoking up the boilers, are we? Maintaining the avoirdupois?'

axe
not ax

axe
is journalese for sack: 'I hated my job at the time and was almost relieved to be axed' isn't convincing.

axes
is the plural of axe and axis.

axis
is used of an alliance of powers, eg Germany and Italy in 1936; the phrase 'axis of evil' was used by George Bush in 2002 of Iraq, Iran and North Korea without any evidence that they were allies.

B

bacteria
is the plural of bacterium and takes a plural verb.

bacterium, bug, microbe, virus
these words all refer to microscopically small living organisms which cause infectious diseases. Bacteria are more complex than viruses. But the biological differences between them are less important than the fact that antibiotics are effective only against bacteria. There are now anti-viral drugs (the best known are the anti-retrovirals used in the treatment of Aids) but they are not antibiotics.

Not all bacteria (or viruses) cause disease, and not all bacterial diseases are easily treated even with antibiotics. Infectious diseases are also caused by other types of organism, eg fungi, protozoa and rickettsia.

Microbe is a non-technical synonym for bacteria and is best avoided. Bug is popular with headline writers ('Flesh-eating bug') but should be kept for certain species of insect.

bail
is confused with bale: bail is security for an accused person; a bail is one of two pieces of wood on top of cricket stumps; also a bucket and a barrier; a bale is a bundle and bale is evil (so baleful). To bail (out) in a boat is to remove water; to bale out of an aircraft is to escape by parachute.

bain *see* bane

20

bait
is confused with bate: bait is food put on a hook to catch fish and to bait is to set a trap or tease; to bate is to lessen (from abate), so bated breath.

bale *see* **bail**

balk
not baulk

balmy
is confused with barmy: balmy, from balm, is fragrant, soothing; barmy, from barm, is fermenting, crazy, so the Barmy Army, England's raucous cricket fans.

bane
cause of misery, is misspelt as bain (French for bath – there is no such word in English):

> Aslef drivers became the bain of commuters for striking.
>
> (*Guardian*)

bank holiday
does not need caps.

barbaric
is confused with barbarous: barbaric is primitive, uncivilised, but with no derogatory implication; barbarous suggests cruel or harsh.

barbecue
not barbeque, bar-b-q or any of the other variants

bare
is confused with bear: bare is naked; a bear is an animal; to bear is to carry.

barrack
whereas in Britain barracking is always hostile, in Australia you can barrack for your team.

base

is confused with bass: base is foundation and, as an adjective, low, whereas bass is the lowest part in music. Musical bass is spoken like base with a long a sound; with a short a bass is a fish.

basically

is a padding word which is hardly ever justified.

bath, bathe

you bath a baby but bathe a wound and bathe in the sea.

bathos

is confused with pathos: bathos is anticlimax, a ludicrous fall from the elevated to the ordinary (after a grand and formal opening the play descended into bathos); pathos is the quality that excites pity or sadness (the play's pathos comes from the hero's inability to understand himself).

bear *see* **bare**

beaus

is the English plural of beau, meaning boyfriend.

Becket, Thomas

the archbishop, not à Becket

Beeton, Mrs

is the correct spelling for the Victorian cookery writer.

befriend

means more than make friends with: it suggests a conscious decision to adopt someone as a friend, and if anything the befriending person has more status. So the following is nonsense:

> I had the honour and pleasure of befriending Susan Sontag – one of the world's greatest writers – in New York.
>
> (Ed Vulliamy, *Observer*)

beg the question *see* **question, beg the**

behove
not behoove

belabour
beat, attack, is confused with labour.

beleagured
is a vogue word for troubled, in difficulty, under pressure of some
kind:

> Britain's beleagured seaside resorts enjoyed a revival yesterday.
> (*Guardian*)

belie
means falsify, conceal; here it's wrongly used to mean reveal:

> Hits like What'd I Say, however, belied another facet of his
> immense talent: his jazz skills.
> (*Guardian*)

benefited, benefiting
etc do not double the t.

bereaved, bereft
to be bereaved is to have lost a family member or partner through
death; to be bereft is to be more generally deprived.

berk *see* **rhyming slang**

best, better *see* **comparative, superlative**

bete noire
literary for bugbear, no longer needs the circumflex accent but it does
need the e on noire; a betise is a blunder.

between
in dates should be followed by 'and', as in 'between 1900 and 1950';
avoid 'between 1900 to 1950' and 'between 1900–1950'.

between you and I
is a mistake: it should be between you and me. Particularly avoid the
following:

> The scene that took place between he and Peter Wheeler ...
> > *(Times)*

See also: **I/me, among**.

beverage
in Britain is a formal word for drinks like tea and Bovril (but see
bevvy, bevy); in the US it's used of drinks in general.

bevvy, bevy
a bevvy is an alcoholic drink; a bevy is a group, eg of women, so 'a
bevvy of naked women disport themselves' is wrong.

biannual, biennial
there is confusion here between twice a year and every two years; it's
safer to spell it out.

biased
not biassed

biennial *see* **biannual, biennial**

billion
use the American billion (a thousand million) not the old-style British
one (a million million).

bimonthly, biweekly
do they mean twice a month/week or every two months/weeks? It's
safer to spell it out.

Biro
is a trade name: use ballpoint pen.

biweekly *see* **bimonthly, biweekly**

black
no cap, is the general word for dark-skinned people, eg those in
Britain of Afro-Caribbean or African descent. Avoid coloured, Negro
– and particularly Negress – except in specialised contexts, eg history.

Black is also used as a term of racial abuse. In 2003 a white Australian
cricketer was banned for using the word to refer to his Sri Lankan
opponents. But afterwards an Aboriginal wrote to the *Australian*:

> I and the rest of my family do not regard being called black
> [as] an insult. In fact we call each other blackfellas and are
> bloody proud to be able to.

See also: **nigger**.

blanch, bleach, blench
they all mean to make or become white; almonds are blanched; clothes
are bleached; and we blench from fear.

blasé
which needs its acute accent, means bored or unimpressed by things
from having seen or experienced them too often.

blatant, flagrant
there is a subtle difference between these two words. As Partridge put
it, 'blatant emphasises the brazenness of the offence and flagrant its
gravity'. A lie, for example, may be blatant if the liar hardly bothers to
conceal the fact that he is lying; a miscarriage of justice may be flagrant
– particularly shocking.

bloc, block
a political group is a bloc; otherwise the word is block.

blond(e)
a man is blond and a woman is blonde; since the word hair has no
gender in English a woman's hair is blond.

bogey, bogie, bogy
are three different words: a bogey (after Colonel Bogey) is a score of one over par at golf; a bogie is a trolley or child's racing cart; a bogy is a goblin or piece of nasal mucus.

bona fides
from Latin is good faith, proof of trustworthiness; bona fide is the adjective, as in 'he is a bona fide traveller'.

bon vivant
is the French for somebody who lives well; bon viveur is an English expression that means the same thing. If you want to sound authentic follow the French.

bored
with or by not of, which is increasingly common:

> he was bored of bed and wanted to impress her.
>
> (Elizabeth Jane Howard)

> Joyce did get rather bored of her.
>
> (Janie Hampton writing about Joyce Grenfell)

borne
from bear, is confused with born as in:

> Her addiction to making porn, rather more dangerously, seems to be borne of the same lack of guile.
>
> (*Weekend Australian Magazine*)

Bosch
the name of a Dutch painter, is confused with Boche, abusive French slang for the Germans:

> the militancy they had honed in the cause of franchise reform was now enlisted in the service of defeating the Bosch.
>
> (*Guardian*)

both

in example after example the word both is redundant:

> Mr Huntley and his girlfriend ... were both being separately
> interviewed by police yesterday.
>
> (*Guardian*)

If two people are being interviewed separately, both adds nothing to
the sense. So too with:

> Both Sailor and Jason Robinson have an infinite regard for
> each other.
>
> (*Times*)

> His parents both died of cancer within a month of one
> another.
>
> (*Observer*)

> Both these programmes have identical target audiences.
>
> (*Sunday Times*)

> They both had ambivalent attitudes in their behaviour to one
> another.
>
> (Elizabeth Jane Howard)

In the following example both is wrong for another reason: it should
refer to two things not three:

> Both Disney, the revisionists ... and the commentators have
> tended to snuff out the life of the tales.
>
> (AS Byatt)

bottle *see* rhyming slang

Boudicca

for the ancient British queen, not Boadicea

breach, breech

breach of promise but breech birth, delivery (so-called because the
buttocks come first)

briar
not brier

bristols *see* **rhyming slang**

brussels sprouts
no cap or apostrophe

bug *see* **bacterium, bug, microbe, virus**

bunch
an American import, means cluster:

> Many non-traditional churches share a bunch of beliefs.
> (*Economist*)

bureau
a writing desk with drawers (but in the US it's a chest of drawers).

bureaux
is the plural of bureau.

burgle
not burglarise (which is American for what a burglar does)

burnt
not burned

bused, busing
not bussed, bussing

busyness
as opposed to business, is used to mean the state of being busy.

but *see* **and, but**

C

caddie, caddy
a caddie carries golf clubs; tea is kept in a caddy.

caesarean (section)
not caesarian or cesarian

café
needs the acute accent.

calendar, calender
a calendar tells you what day it is; a calender is a rolling machine for paper or cloth.

callous, callus
callous is cruel; a callus is hard skin.

campbed
one word

can *see* **may, can, might**

cannon, canon
a cannon is a large gun and a double-touching stroke in billiards; a canon is a law or rule and a clergyman. In the literary sense the canon is (a list of) the recognised works of an individual writer or established writers in general:

> Smollett has faded from syllabuses even as the academic canon has expanded.
>
> (*Guardian*)

Canute (King)

not Cnut or Knut. According to tradition, Canute's purpose in commanding the tide to stop coming in was to show his courtiers he was not omnipotent – most people get this story mixed up; see **clichés**.

canvas, canvass

canvas is cloth, whether for sails, tents or paintings; to canvass is to solicit votes.

capital, capitol

the spelling is always capital, except for the building where American legislatures meet.

capsize

a rare –ize spelling in British English.

carat, caret

a carat is a unit of measurement for gold and gems; a caret is an insertion mark in proofreading.

carcass, carcasses

not carcase, carcases

careen

turn a ship on its side for cleaning or repair, is confused with career, rush headlong.

cashmere, Kashmir

cashmere is a fine, soft fabric made from Kashmiri goats' hair.

castor

not caster for a small wheel on a piece of furniture, a sugar sprinkler and fine sugar, the beaver and castor oil

casus belli

not causus: an act seen as a reason for war, not its cause. But Andrew Motion wrote a short poem in 2003 called 'Causa belli', referring to the causes of war.

cat

its slang meaning changes from Britain to the US:

> Their only meeting with the US media ended in confusion.
> 'He kept calling us cats,' frowns Oxide. 'Where we come from
> cat means crackhead.'
>
> *(Guardian)*

catapult

not catapault

Catholic

with a cap and without qualification means Roman Catholic; without
a cap it means common, general, tolerant. As the Catholic writer
Anthony Burgess said, 'I've got catholic tastes. Catholic with a small
"c" of course.'

cause célèbre

something to campaign for, not against, as here:

> Elected officials ... have made under-age drinking a cause
> célèbre in Westchester.
>
> *(New York Times)*

caviar

not caviare for sturgeon's roe

celebrant, celebrator

a celebrant says Mass; a celebrator makes merry.

Celeste, Mary *see* **Mary Celeste**

celibate

is used to mean both unmarried (its original meaning) and abstaining
from sex. In the case of gays celibate almost always means abstaining
from sex:

> I give thanks to God for being gay. I am not exactly celibate.
>
> *(Times)*

So too with married people. *A Celibate Season* is the title of a novel by Carol Shields and Blanche Howard, which tells the story of a married couple and their self-imposed 10-month separation.

In some cases celibate is added to unmarried, making it clear that the addition refers to sex not marriage:

> He has never married, and has apparently been celibate for years.
>
> *(Guardian)*

> Why did he [Cliff Richard] never marry? Is he gay? Is he celibate?
>
> *(Radio Times)*

But the original meaning of the word has not disappeared:

> Pressure to relax the celibacy rule for Roman Catholic priests is growing as increasing numbers of former Anglican vicars work successfully in Catholic parishes.
>
> *(Times)*

> Priests felt well-prepared for public ministry, remained faithful to the discipline of daily prayer and Mass, and had high regard for chastity and celibacy.
>
> *(Times)*

In some cases there is confusion between the two meanings. What does celibacy mean in the following example?

> He voluntarily gave up the priesthood, retaining a commitment to celibacy.
>
> *(Times)*

And in this?

> There has been little understanding of the source of abuse: paedophiles' exploitation of the power and authority of the

priesthood and their convenient though erroneous belief that
sexually tampering with children does not necessarily undermine vows of celibacy.

(Stephen Bates, religious correspondent of the *Guardian*)

But to be precise: a paedophile priest who sexually abuses children
does not break his vow of celibacy since he remains unmarried. You
would think the religious correspondent of the *Guardian* would know
this, and would avoid confusing the issue. Where celibacy still has the
formal meaning of the unmarried state, as with Catholic priests, it
shouldn't be used for abstaining from sex.

celsius, centigrade
two words for the thermometer constructed by Celsius; prefer celsius.

censer, censor, censure
a censer is a pan in which incense is burnt; a censor has power to
suppress material; censure is blame.

centre in, on
not around

centrifugal, centripetal
centrifugal force pulls away from the centre; centripetal pulls towards
it.

cereal
grain, is confused with serial, forming a series.

chacun à son gout
is not French but franglais; the French expression is (*à*) *chacun son gout*.

chaff
tease, is confused with chafe, irritate, as in this reference to an actress
wearing body jewellery:

We only hope it didn't chaff.
(*Guardian*)

chair, chairman, chairwoman

a chairman or chairwoman takes the chair at a meeting; a person cannot be a chair. *See also*: **-person**.

chaperon(e)

although, strictly speaking, the French word chaperon is a masculine noun, in English the feminine form chaperone has replaced it. So an older woman chaperones/acts as chaperone to a young woman.

chaser

a long drink, usually beer, which follows a tot of spirits (though the word is also used of spirits after beer).

chaste

the original word meaning abstaining from sex:

> A small number of members [of Opus Dei] take vows of chastity, live in sex-segregated communities and give much of their income to Opus.
>
> (*Guardian*)

> Fr Mantero said he discovered he was gay when he fell in love with a man eight years ago. He stuck to his vows of chastity, however, until two years ago.
>
> (*Guardian*)

chateau, chateaux

the circumflex accent is not necessary.

chauffeured

not chauffered

chauvinist

an extreme nationalist (from the fictional character Nicolas Chauvin, one of Napoleon's veterans), an excessive advocate of any cause or – the most common meaning today – a sexist (originally male chauvinist pig).

cheddar, cheshire cheese
no caps

chips
in Britain are chipped potatoes, whereas in the US and France chips are what the British call crisps; in Australia it may say crisps on the packet but everybody calls them chips, so chipped potatoes have to be 'hot chips'.

chord, cord
a chord is a group of musical notes; a cord is a length of rope; you sing chords with your vocal cords.

Christ Church
the Oxford college, does not have the word college in its title.

chronic *see* **acute**

church, the
no caps whether Catholic or Anglican

circumlocution
saying things in a roundabout way: 'with regard to' instead of 'about'.

circumstances
in the, not under the

City, the
with cap, for London's financial centre

classic, classical
the classics are Greek and Latin language and literature; classical refers to Greek and Roman culture and is the opposite of romantic; classic is used of anything outstanding, definitive or stylish including the five chief races in the English flat-racing season.

cleave
means both to split and to stick; see **opposite meanings**.

clichés

the style books rightly say you should try to avoid a string of clichés as in:

> A creative dynamo in her own right, a sharp businesswoman and consumed by a burning desire to make sure that the show went on, the slain fashion guru's larger-than-life platinum-haired sister was the obvious choice to don the mantle.
>
> (profile of Donatella Versace, sister of the slain Gianni, *Hello!*)

It's difficult to write without using the occasional cliché. But there are certain key mistakes to avoid. First, don't get your cliché wrong. References to King Canute, Lord Copper and Hobson's choice are usually wrong: that is, they distort the meaning of the original phrase or anecdote.

Here's a double distortion: 'What we did eat was a parson's egg – good in parts' (AA Gill in the *Sunday Times* 'Style' section). First, it was a curate not a parson. Second, the point of the story is that the egg was bad though the curate was politely reluctant to admit it. In the original *Punch* cartoon the bishop says to the curate: 'I'm afraid you've got a bad egg, Mr Jones.' The curate replies: 'Oh no, my lord, I assure you! Parts of it are excellent!'

A second point follows. Since most people get the curate's egg wrong, it's pretty silly in most contexts to use it at all. Is 'a curate's egg of a book' a mixture of good and bad – or a thoroughly bad one that for some reason you decide to be euphemistic about?

Also, if you do use a cliché, have the courage of your convictions: don't apologise or struggle to justify your decision. This only makes matters worse since the reader becomes more aware of what you're doing. Here are some examples of what not to do:

> For once it is legitimate to use the hoary cliché that Irish rugby will never see his like again.
>
> (Peter Clohessy as seen by Robert Kitson, *Guardian*)

> Her face was, forgive the cliché, heart-shaped.
>
> (Zina Rohan)

> Russia jumped the gun (forgive the expression).
>
> (*Economist*)

climactic, climatic, climacteric

climactic refers to a climax; climatic to the weather; climacteric to a critical period in human life.

clippings

is American for (press) cuttings.

cobblers *see* rhyming slang

cohort

means both an individual supporter and a group of like-minded people:

> Punk was dead within a couple of years, as was Rotten's cohort, Sid Vicious.
>
> *(Guardian)*

> a cohort of desperately hungry politicians.
> *(Guardian)*

But what does cohorts mean here?

> As for language, television and its cohorts have had the direst effect on adjectives.
>
> (Nick Clarke)

Is it 'other media, eg tabloid newspapers' or 'the people who work in television'?

Cohort is also confused with consort, partner:

> She [Cherie Blair] is clearly ashamed, as both she and her prime ministerial cohort should be.
>
> *(Guardian)*

A word to avoid.

collateral damage *see* euphemism

collective nouns

in English take either a singular or a plural verb, eg 'The team is small' (it consists of few people) but 'The team are small' (they are not very tall). See **number agreement**.

combat, combated, combating

are the recommended spellings but fight is a better verb.

come

is confused with cum (with): 'a museum come delicatessen'.

comic, comical

comic refers to comedy, as in comic opera; comical is funny, ridiculous.

commence

although Hemingway used it, is formal for start, begin.

commit

is now often used with the object understood:

> Will he commit to accept its recommendations?
> (*Guardian*)

> The government must commit to the new protocol.
> (*Guardian* letter)

commonsense

is now one word for the noun as well as the adjective.

commute

which originally meant to travel to work by season ticket, now includes any daily journey – but not intercontinental travel:

> Thornton will commute to China from the $18m Georgian mansion set in 118 acres of New Jersey that he recently bought.
> (*Guardian*)

comparative, superlative

people often use the superlative (best) when the comparative (better) would be better. You can't logically have the best of two, only the best of three or more. And you can only get the better, not the best, of someone. So Booker prizewinner Yann Martel is wrong to write: 'Mrs Gandhi finally got the best of Father.' To get the best of someone would be to benefit from them (though you can best them).

And Donna Tartt is wrong to use the superlative in this reference to Cinderella's two stepsisters: 'Harriet was the smallest – and the meanest – of the wicked stepsisters.' It should be 'the smaller – and the meaner'.

comparatively, relatively

should only be used when some comparison is made: 'He is comparatively/relatively small/rich etc' needs a reference point.

compare to, with

the traditional distinction is clear: you compare like with like, last year's figures with this year's; when you compare something to something else ('Shall I compare thee to a summer's day?'), you liken the two things: you stress aspects they have in common. The distinction is useful but many people now use to in both senses.

A mistake to be avoided is to compare this year's figures with last year or France's exports with Germany.

complaisant, compliant, complacent

complaisant is obliging, ready to condone; compliant is yielding; complacent is smug, self-satisfied.

complement, compliment

to complement is to complete or make whole; to compliment is to praise.

comprehensible, comprehensive

comprehensible is understandable; comprehensive is inclusive.

comprise

is formal for consist of; comprise of and is comprised of are both wrong. When an estate agent says, 'The accommodation comprises of/is comprised of four rooms', it should be 'The accommodation comprises four rooms.'

compulsive, compulsory
compulsive behaviour, eg lying, results from an inner compulsion; compulsory means imposed by someone else.

compunction
means more than reluctance: it means remorse tinged with pity. So the following is wrong:

> He has no compunction in nominating Campbell.
> *(Guardian)*

concerned
means either worried or involved: worried if it comes before the noun, involved if it comes after it. So the following is wrong:

> Other concerned staff have received goods.
> *(Observer)*

concert, consort
concert means agreement or harmony; a consort is a companion or partner; so the following is wrong:

> Frail as any paper my parents were fading in consort.
> (Zina Rohan)

concord *see* agreement

confidant(e)
a male or female friend to be trusted with private information.

congenital, genetic/hereditary
inherited conditions are genetic or hereditary; congenital conditions date from birth.

conjugal, connubial

are literary for relating to marriage. 'Conducting conjugal relations' is a euphemism for having sex.

connection

not connexion

consensus

not concensus, does not need 'general' before it or 'of opinion' after it: consensus means the general opinion so the word 'general' is wasted in:

> There's a general public consensus that prison doesn't really work.
>
> *(Sunday Times)*

consummate

as an adjective, means complete, perfect; often misused.

contagious, infectious

contagious diseases are spread by touching; infectious diseases through the air or water, particularly by bacteria and viruses. See **bacterium, bug, microbe, virus**.

contemporary

is used to mean both belonging to the same time and modern, present-day. In the following example it isn't clear which meaning is intended:

> The current mayor ... bristled when I suggested that there was necessarily such a component in contemporary judgements of the regime.
>
> (Adam Nossiter)

contemptible, contemptuous

contemptible means despicable; contemptuous means scornful.

continual, continuous

if it rains continually it rains a lot but sometimes stops; if it rains continuously it goes on raining all the time. Which is this?

> Despite working continually, 43-year-old Pearson's star has waned a little.
>
> *(Guardian)*

convener

not convenor

co-respondent, correspondent

a co-respondent features in a divorce case; a correspondent writes letters or newspaper articles.

cornish pasty

no cap

corps, corpse, corpus

a corps is an organised group of people; a corpse is a dead body; a corpus is a collection of, eg, writings.

coruscate

sparkle, is confused with excoriate, strip the skin from, criticise severely.

cot

in Britain a cot is a high-sided bed for babies and small children; in the US it is a campbed.

council, counsel

a council is an advisory or administrative body; counsel is advice and opinion; also a barrister or advocate (the Scottish equivalent); a councillor is a member of a council; a counsellor provides counselling, organised therapeutic advice.

coup, coupe, coupé

a coup is a blow or strike; a coupe is a shallow dish (and the dessert inside it); a coupé is a two-door car with a sloping roof; in the US the coupé loses its accent.

court martial

for the noun, plural courts martial, but to court-martial.

cow

is confused with kowtow, the Chinese word for prostrating yourself:

> He may have been exasperated by the UN Security Council's refusal to cow before his friends in Washington.
>
> *(Times)*

cower

is confused with cow:

> We were a people cowered by English culture.
> (Australian Richard Flanagan)

credible, credulous, creditable

credible is believable; credulous is easily taken in; creditable is trustworthy or praiseworthy.

crescendo

is, correctly, the rising of a sound towards a climax, rather than the climax itself, so the following is a misuse:

> If he's right, the criticisms could rapidly rise to a crescendo.
>
> *(Guardian)*

crevasse, crevice

a crevice is a narrow opening in rock; a crevasse is a much bigger fissure in a glacier or river bank.

criteria, criterion

criterion, means or standard of judging, is the singular of criteria:

The common criterion for academic success is exam performance.

culs–de–sac
is the plural of cul–de–sac.

cumberland sausage
no cap

curate's egg *see* clichés

curb, kerb
a curb is a check or restraint and the American spelling for kerb, the edge of a pavement (which in the US is a sidewalk).

currant, current
a currant is a small black raisin; a current is a stream or flow of electricity.

currently
is a padding word which is hardly ever justified: use now (or nothing).

cut back, cutback
to cut back and cutback, the noun, are elaborate and pointless ways of saying cut.

D

dangling modifiers

The dangling modifier is a curse of modern writing, particularly obituaries. In many cases the dangling modifier is a participle (also called floating):

> Having started out with insouciance and recklessness that masked heroism, her later life was a long anti-climax.

Literally this says that it was her later life that started out 'with insouciance and recklessness', which does not make sense, although the reader can usually make sense of it.

Sometimes the dangling modifier makes perfect sense but distorts the writer's meaning:

> Born in Brixton, his father was a trapeze artist.

Literally this says that it was the father that was born in Brixton, which is not what the writer wants to say at all.

To avoid making this error always ensure that a participle at the beginning of a sentence has the same subject as the main clause that follows. So in the second sentence 'Born in Brixton' must be followed by the person who was actually born there.

What about common expressions like 'generally speaking' or 'putting two and two together'? These are not considered to be dangling because the unexpressed subject is indefinite (one, people in general). 'Putting two and two together, it's clear he's guilty' is equivalent to saying 'If one puts two and two together, it's clear he's guilty.'

A similar argument applies to adverbs like presumably, thankfully and hopefully. They are dropped into a sentence with the general effect of 'one presumes', 'one is thankful' and 'one hopes'.

Thus there is no grammatical problem with expressions like 'generally speaking' and 'hopefully'; they have usefully replaced the stilted 'one' construction. But there can be stylistic objections – see **hopefully** and **sentence adverbs**.

dash
since the dash is such a strong stop it's a useful rule of thumb that you should never put more than two in a sentence. Also, if there are two, they should be used to mark a parenthesis.

data
is, strictly speaking, a plural but the singular datum sounds pedantic as in 'a datum relating to my memory' (Saul Bellow). Advice: use data but try to avoid following it with a singular verb.

dates
prefer 8 November 1977, that is day, month, year. This is more logical (because it is a sequence) than month, day, year and also needs no commas, whereas in November 8 1977 a comma would be needed to separate the two figures. There is no need for th after 8. The American style is to put the month before the day, hence 9/11 and September 11 for the attack on the World Trade Centre.

daughters-in-law
is the plural of daughter-in-law.

deadly, deathly
deadly is fatal, causing death; deathly is a poetical word meaning deathlike, pale.

debatable
not debateable

decimate
What does this word mean today? Its origin is not in doubt: it comes from the Latin for kill every tenth man, the Roman army's vicious punishment. The horrific and arbitrary nature of this reprisal has

pushed the word in the direction of massacre, destroy, reduce heavily. But the idea of a minority being killed as opposed to a majority hasn't totally disappeared:

> The people faced these events with stoicism. When a shell decimated a line of women queuing for food, their ranks closed to fill the gap.
>
> (*Observer*)

And here's an example where the writer has certainly tried to get it right:

> Ireland's population was literally decimated: one in every eight Irishmen – a million people – died of starvation in three years.
> (Michael Pollan)

But, sadly, Pollan's arithmetic has let him down – one in eight is more than one in ten (and 'literally' makes 'decimated' even worse).

In general you would expect historians to be precise in their use of decimate, particularly if they are writing about the Roman army or the German occupying army of the 1940s, notorious for reprisals against civilians which in some cases were based on the one-in-10 principle. But in the following examples how many people are killed?

> The Gestapo decimated Libération-Nord in September 1943.

> Royer's network remained ignorant of the threat and was decimated.
>
> (both by Robert Gildea)

We may be able to guess the answer from the context; without it we are lost.

The commonest modern meaning of decimate is destroy:

> The seat Alexis was sitting in only hours before this latest crash was completely decimated.
>
> (*Australian*)

> His theory would decimate conventional exams.
> (*Sunday Times*)

Indeed the two words destroy and decimate are sometimes used as alternatives in the same sentence:

> Entire streets were decimated and lives destroyed.
> *(Australian)*

You could equally destroy the streets and decimate the lives.

Then there is the light-hearted, facetious use of decimate instead of, say, devastate:

> One can't help wondering whether Cooper would have been quite so appreciative of their exquisite good looks and decimating sex appeal ... if they'd been, say, binmen.
> *(Sunday Times)*

> Shorts rolled up, legs in the air, decimated picnic.
> (Zadie Smith)

We are a long way from the horror of the Roman execution squad; surely it's time to bury the word decimate.

decry, descry
decry is belittle; descry is literary for catch sight of.

deduce, deduct
deduce is infer by reasoning; deduct is subtract.

defective, deficient
defective is faulty; deficient is lacking in something.

definite, definitive
definite is precise; definitive is final and conclusive.

defuse, diffuse
defuse is make harmless; to diffuse is to spread and diffuse as an adjective means widely spread or wordy.

deja vu

which does not need accents, can mean either the illusory feeling of having experienced something before or the correct impression that this is so, hence tedious familiarity.

delink

is an American variant of not link, unlink:

> If an invasion of Iraq is delinked from Middle East peace ...
> *(New York Times)*

But there is an obvious and important difference between not link (to) and unlink (from): the first assumes that a link does not exist; the second that it does. So delink should be avoided on the grounds of ambiguity.

deliver

doctors and midwives do not deliver babies (though storks could be said to); they deliver mothers of their babies.

delusion, illusion

delusion is false belief or hallucination (delusions of grandeur); illusion is false impression (optical illusion).

demise

a lawyer's word, is pretentious for death; it does not mean decline.

denizen

is literary for inhabitant, occupant:

> The denizens of Fleet Street.
> *(Daily Telegraph)*

denouement

does not need an accent.

dent, dint

two spellings of the same word meaning the hollow caused by a blow (and originally the blow itself); 'by dint of' is literary for 'by means of'.

dependant, dependent

dependant is the noun, dependent the adjective, so dependence.

deprecate, depreciate

deprecate is deplore, protest against; depreciate, the opposite of appreciate, means both disparage and fall in value. Here it means disparage:

> His work has to be seen to be depreciated.
> *(Sunday Times)*

de rigueur

strictly required, has the letter u twice.

derisive, derisory

derisive is mocking; derisory is laughable.

Derry *see* Londonderry

descendant

is confused with ancestor/forebear:

> But who were these first peoples? Scientists assumed they were descendants of native Americans who now claim ownership of ancient human remains.
> *(Guardian)*

See **mirror words**.

deserts, desserts

the common confusion here is not between deserts (sandy places) and desserts (puddings) but between them and deserts (what is deserved, as in 'he received his just deserts').

déshabillé

not dishabille, has traditionally meant not nudity but the state of being partly dressed (and a déshabillé is another word for a négligé, a woman's light dressing-gown):

> Backstage the actress signed autographs in déshabillé.

So the following is wrong:

> The boy who spotted the emperor's déshabillé.
> (*Independent*)

In the story the emperor is wearing nothing at all.

detente
does not need an accent.

detract, distract
detract is take away; distract is divert the attention of.

device, devise
device is the noun, devise the verb.

dextrous
not dexterous

dice, die
dice is the plural of die, the small cube with numbered faces used in gambling and board games. Dice has replaced die in most contexts (so it is both singular and plural) but die survives in stock phrases like straight as a die and the die is cast.

dicey
not dicy

dietitian
not dietician

different

is used as a padding word:

> On holiday we went to various different places.

It is also used to replace various:

> On holiday we went to different places.

Prefer various by itself.

different from, than, to

should it be different from, than or to or doesn't it matter? Where different is linked to a noun or pronoun by a preposition British usage traditionally prefers from:

> The British are different from the Americans.

But to is much more common:

> The British are different to them.

Some people prefer from because it is consistent with differs from:

> The British differ from the Americans.

Others prefer to because it is consistent with indifferent to:

> The British are indifferent to them.

In American usage from is traditionally recommended by the experts, eg Strunk and White, but than is clearly dominant:

> The Americans are different than the British.

Advice: use 'than' if you want your writing to have an American accent; otherwise use 'from' to be formal and 'to' to be informal. But if there is no ambiguity, it doesn't matter very much whether you use 'from' or 'to'.

The position is complicated when different becomes differently or forms part of a more elaborate phrase or clause:

> The Normans went hunting and spoke differently/in a different language to the peasants.

Is this 'they spoke in a different way from the peasants (ie the Normans spoke French, while the peasants spoke Anglo-Saxon)'? Or is it 'they spoke to the peasants in a different way from their usual one (ie they made an effort to speak Anglo-Saxon)'?

Advice: don't use 'to' when there's a risk of ambiguity.

For clauses Bryson recommends 'than', quoting John Maynard Keynes:

> How different things appear in Washington than in London.

Salman Rushdie agrees:

> I find my tongue doing slightly different things with Urdu than I do 'with ... your tongue down my throat'.

But for most British writers 'different than' suggests degrees of difference. To put different and than together you would need something like:

> The British are more different from the Americans than the Germans are from the French.

Advice: in British English don't use different than.

differ from, with
to differ from is merely to be different; to differ with is to disagree.

dike *see* dyke

dilemma
a dilemma is more than an awkward problem. Strictly speaking it means a choice between two alternatives both of which are undesirable:

A woman who faced the classic career woman's dilemma
(whether to sacrifice time at work or time with the family).

(*Daily Mail*)

It's risky not to check your facts; but risky to check as well.
Here on the Diary we know the dilemma well.

(*Guardian*)

The word can reasonably be extended to cover more than two
unattractive choices but it should not be used as a literary variation
word for problem:

Our dilemma in modern times is that we are around for heart
disease and cancer to enter the equation.

(*Times*)

There are countless spells to be had for every occasion and
dilemma.

(*Guardian*)

dinghy, dingy
a dinghy is a small rowing-boat; dingy is dark-coloured or dirty.

dint *see* **dent, dint**

diphtheria
not diptheria

diplomat
not diplomatist

disassemble, dissemble
disassemble is take to pieces; dissemble is disguise, deceive.

disassociate *see* **dissociate**

disastrous
not disasterous

disc, disk
disc for all non-computer uses; disk for computers.

discernible
not discernable

discomfit, discomfort
discomfit is an old word meaning defeat:

> Now here I was, weakened, discomfited and – the phrase
> occurred to me – at her mercy.
> (Zina Rohan)

But it's often used now to mean something like make uncomfortable:

> Harmison discomfited all Australia's top-order batsmen.
> (Australian cricketer Tom Moody)

> The Peat inquiry evidently has the capacity to discomfit
> Prince Charles too.
> (*Observer*)

It would be better to use discomfort in the cases above, as Rod Liddle
has done here:

> Bennett's behaviour discomforted the student body.

discreet, discrete
discreet means tactful, judicious; discrete means distinct, separate; but
being discreet is discretion; the noun from discrete is discreteness.

disfranchise
not disenfranchise

disinterest, disinterested
have the traditional meanings of impartiality, impartial, but are more
commonly used to mean lack of interest, uninterested:

So how would she be spending her time meanwhile? Joseph asked with splendid disinterest.

(John Le Carré)

Brought up on state pensions and benefits by her Conservative-voting, though politically disinterested, grand-parents.

(*Guardian*)

'Why?' she asked with apparent disinterest, as if he were talking about someone else.

(translator Margaret Jull Costa)

Advice: most uses of disinterested risk confusion – use impartial or bored.

disk *see* **disc, disk**

disorient, disorientate *see* **orient, orientate**

dispatch
not despatch

dissociate
not disassociate; dissociate from not with.

distaste for
not of

distrait, distraught
distrait means absent-minded; distraught means upset.

dived *see* **dove**

divers, diverse
divers is archaic for several; diverse means varied.

divorcee
for both sexes, not divorcé(e)

dog days
After the *Guardian* used the headline 'Dog days for the dollar' to mean troubled times, they apologised, saying that according to Collins dog days are neutral. But Oxford disagrees:

> Traditionally regarded as the hottest and unhealthiest time of the year; *fig.* a period in which malignant influences prevail.
>
> *(New Shorter Oxford)*

Follow Oxford: dog days are bad news.

dos and don'ts
which once had three apostrophes, now needs only one.

dotcom
not dot-com or dot.com – the second is particularly silly, since it means dotdotcom or ..com.

double entendre
this is an English expression (the French is *double entente*) for a phrase with two meanings, one of them indecent. By contrast double meaning merely suggests ambiguity.

double negative
there is a clear difference between the standard form of English and its dialects in the use of the double negative. In dialect English a second negative reinforces the first:

> I can't get no satisfaction.
> (singer Mick Jagger)

> Mike Tyson doesn't have no honour in that sense to me.
> (boxer Lennox Lewis)

But in standard English a second negative contradicts the first to make a positive:

> It's not unusual ...
>> (singer Tom Jones)

> It's not as if Danny and Ben are not world-class second-rows.
>> (rugby player Martin Johnson)

In the right hands it can be a subtle literary device:

> She always camped in the bush, alone – and was never not in a hurry.
>> (Bruce Chatwin)

> Nobody who dealt in money did not wear stockings.
>> (Jonathan Frantzen)

But it can also be clumsy and confusing:

> This is not to say that the bulk of honours should not go to people ... of whom we might otherwise never hear.
>> (Robert Harris)

> It is hard to deny that Pinker ... is not on to a good thing.
>> (*Observer*)

In the second example the writer wants to say that Pinker is probably on to a good thing – but has in fact said the opposite. With both you have to stop and try to puzzle out the meaning.

Advice: use the double negative with care to assert a positive; don't use it (except informally) to emphasise a negative.

double superlative
avoid following one superlative by another:

> Yet if they are an incomplete and misleading source, they are the least worst.
>> (*Guardian*)

dove

a dove is a bird; dove (pronounced as in stove) is an American variant of dived; it shows no signs of catching on in Britain.

dover sole

needs no cap.

downmarket

is marketing jargon for products and services that are cheap and lacking in style and prestige; by extension it's used to mean vulgar in general:

> I can see why he's attractive to a certain kind of woman with his slightly downmarket playboy looks.
>
> (*Evening Standard*)

downsizing *see* euphemism

draconian

from Draco of Athens, meaning very severe, needs no cap.

draft, draught

draft is used for selection (eg conscription), a bank order and a preliminary sketch or version; draught for something drawn, pulled or drunk, a current of air and the depth to which a ship sinks in the water.

dreamt

not dreamed ('I dreamt that I dwelt in marble halls', Alfred Bunn)

drier, dryer

drier, driest are the comparative and superlative of dry; use dryer for hair.

drily

not dryly

driving licence
is British; driver's license is American.

dryer *see* **drier, dryer**

dual *see* **duel**

dudgeon
is literary for indignation, resentment:

> He had his dudgeons.
> (Saul Bellow)

duel
is confused with dual:

> A highly collectable duel-function ... candlestick-cum-rose vase.
>
> (*Guardian*)

due to
traditionally 'due to' could not be substituted for 'because of' in sentences like: 'The match was cancelled because of bad weather' (though 'owing to' was an acceptable alternative).

This was because due, as an adjective, had to refer to a noun as in: 'The cancellation of the match was due to bad weather.'

The loose, adverbial use of due to is now accepted by some but still criticised by others. A *Guardian* reader's letter said that the poor quality of JK Rowling's English in the Harry Potter books was illustrated by the second sentence of *Harry Potter and the Order of the Phoenix*:

> The use of hosepipes had been banned due to drought.

So it's safer to use 'because of'.

duffel
not duffle

dumb

for stupid is now mainstream British English.

Durex

which in Britain is a condom, is sticky tape in Australia and Brazil.

dwarfs

not dwarves, although the scholarly Tolkien uses dwarves. Kate Burridge says that the plural was always dwarfs but that dwarves may have been adopted in fairy stories because of the influence of words like elves and wolves. Tolkien took this view 'even though as a philologist he knew this was historically wrong'. Stick to dwarfs.

dyeing, dying

dyeing is staining, changing the colour of something; dying is ending life.

dyke

not dike in all senses

dysphoric

is literary for painful:

> The process of dismemberment is a deeply weird and dysphoric experience.
>
> (*Guardian*)

E

earned
not earnt

earring
not ear-ring

eclair, eclat
don't need accents.

economic, economical
economic is to do with economics or business or likely to be profitable; economical is thrifty or cheap.

ecstasy
not ecstacy

educationist
not educationalist

effect *see* **affect, effect**

effete
literally means worn out (from giving birth) but it is also used (of men) as a variant of effeminate, soft and decadent:

> Eden displayed a fastidiousness – not just about his appearance – that many found effete.
>
> (RW Johnson, *London Review of Books*)

Best avoided.

eg

which is short for the Latin *exempli gratia* meaning for example, does not need full stops or a comma after it.

egoist, egotist

egoism is a philosophical theory; egotism is selfishness, hence egotistical.

egregious

from the Latin *egregius*, chosen out of the flock, always means exceptional; the problem is that it can be used in either a positive or a negative sense. According to Chambers, the positive sense is archaic but here are two modern examples (both from Australian writers):

> Unlike the US, Australia believed that it was not a matter of egregious enterprise by an individual that should determine his welfare.
>
> (Thomas Keneally)

> What we are seeing here is a case of linguistic steam-rolling by that egregiously successful little ending –s.
>
> (Kate Burridge)

The negative sense is far more common:

> I was never broody thanks to a particularly egregious younger brother.
>
> (scientist Susan Greenfield)

> Chip stood in the middle of the room with a towel round his waist. He felt warty and egregious. He felt that Melissa was right to be disgusted by him.
>
> (Jonathan Frantzen)

> Peter Gladwin should be congratulated for making an egregious vegetable like mangetout even more dislikable.
>
> (Fay Maschler)

In these examples egregious is a literary way of saying 'exceptionally unpleasant'. But it's lazy because it isn't specific. Even worse, the word is sometimes used negatively of a group of people, thus losing the sense of exceptional:

> The egregious members of the Test and County Cricket Board.
>
> (Frances Edmonds)

A word to avoid, unless you are seeking to impress rather than communicate.

eirenic
is literary for peaceful:

> Noam Chomsky rails against Bush's war on terror from within the eirenic environs of the MIT.
>
> (TV producer Tristram Hunt)

either, neither
refer emphatically to two possibilities: either go or stay; neither one thing nor the other. Either is followed by or, neither by nor (so neither ... or is wrong). The point is to emphasise that there is a choice between two. Burchfield quotes (without condemning) some examples of more than two:

> Either France or Germany or Italy will break ranks in the matter.

> Neither ABC nor CBS nor NBC has a permanent team in black Africa.
>
> (*New Yorker*)

But there is a difference between 'either France or Germany or Italy' and 'either France, Germany or Italy'. The first makes some use of the essentially dual nature of either (A or B, B or C); the second ignores it. So do not write 'Come on either Friday, Saturday or Sunday'. Either has no function here. But you could write 'Come on either Friday or Saturday – or Sunday, if you prefer.'

These examples confirm that both either and neither have much more force when used of two possibilities.

As subjects either and neither are usually followed by a singular verb:

Either of these routes is possible.

Neither one thing nor the other pleases him.

But where the second subject (ie the one nearer the verb) is plural, the verb becomes plural:

I heard a car. Either the captain or two of his players have arrived.

If the first subject is plural but the second singular, the verb remains singular:

Either the players or their captain has arrived.

The subject nearer the verb governs it in other ways too:

Neither you nor he has spoken.

Neither he nor you have spoken.

In speech and informal writing a plural verb is sometimes used even where both subjects are singular:

Have either of them turned up yet?

But in formal writing it's better to stick to the singular has.

Either and neither should be put in the right place, which is before the part of the sentence they refer to: 'In this example either the grammar is incorrect or informal' is wrong: either should go before incorrect.

Either can sometimes be substituted for each:

There are trees on either side of the road.

But not if there is a risk of ambiguity: 'Trams run on either side of the road' could mean on both sides or on one. To be clear use each/one.

Just as neither must be followed by nor or not it can't be combined with a positive:

> It was an unusual form of seating, but then, neither was the garden of the usual kind.
>
> (Beryl Bainbridge)

Unusual may have a negative meaning but it has a positive form: for 'neither' to work 'it was an unusual' would have to be 'it was not a usual'.

eke out
the traditional meaning of eke out is to make something go further: 'He eked out his supplies by picking wild fruit.'

But the word is now more commonly used to mean to achieve something with difficulty:

> The recovery from 10–0 down in Huddersfield is the basis for Britain to eke out the victory they desperately require.
>
> (*Times*)

elan
doesn't need an accent.

elder, older
elder is now the noun, older the adjective; but elder is still used as an adjective in certain contexts, eg 'his elder brother', 'an elder statesman'.

elderly
according to the dictionary elderly means quite old, on the way to being old, etc – but its most common use is as a euphemism: 'the elderly', like 'senior citizens', is now a polite and patronising way of

saying 'old people'. For this reason it's likely to cause offence when used to mean 'quite old'. A newspaper report calling two people aged 61 and 62 'an elderly couple' was not popular with readers in their sixties.

elegant variation *see* variation

elegy, eulogy
an elegy is a mournful poem; a eulogy is a tribute to someone alive or dead.

elemental, elementary
elemental is connected with the elements; elementary is simple or rudimentary.

elicit, illicit
to elicit is to draw out; illicit is an adjective meaning illegal.

elite
doesn't need an accent.

elusive *see* allusive.

email
but e-fit, etc.

embarrass
unlike harass, has two r's.

embed
(eg for journalist serving with the military) not imbed

emblematic
is literary for symbolic:

> Morris's return to the backbenches is emblematic.
> (*Guardian*)

embonpoint

is a French word meaning plumpness (*en bon point*) which has become a vogue word for large breasts:

> An extraordinarily attractive blonde woman called Lee was promoted to alpha female in the time it took her embonpoint to enter the room.
>
> (Times)

emend, amend

emend is remove errors in a text; amend is improve.

émigré

needs both acute accents: see **accents**

emollience

is pretentious for softness, as in this reference to being nice to Madonna (echoing the phrase 'fair, fine, soft words butter no parsnips'):

> Such emollience has buttered no parsnips in the Material Girl's camp.
>
> (Sunday Times)

employee

not employé for employed person

encyclopedia

not encyclopaedia

endemic

is a technical term in biology and medicine which means regularly found; it's also a vogue word for prevalent:

> The endemic sexism that permeates New Labour.
>
> (Guardian)

enormity, enormous, enormousness

enormous is used to mean either immense or excessive or both. 'He went to enormous trouble' means that he worked very hard - and should be praised rather than criticised for doing so - whereas 'he has an enormous head' suggests a lack of proportion. Enormousness means great size but it is a clumsy word, usually replaced by enormity:

> 'That evening ... he had reflected on the enormity of his good fortune.'
> (Alexander McCall Smith)

The trouble is that enormity also means great wickedness, as in 'the enormities of their conduct' and 'the enormity of his crime'. And some experts, eg Bryson and Trask, insist that it should be used only in this way.

Advice: use enormity with care.

enquire/y *see* inquire/y

ensure, insure

ensure (make certain) is contrasted with insure (protect something against financial loss) in British English; in the US insure is used for both.

entrance, entry

there are various differences in usage between these two similar words: an entrance fee is charged for admission, eg to performances; if an owner refuses admittance, eg to a path, a sign might read 'No entry'.

entrée

originally an intermediate course in elaborate menus – not starting the meal but preparing the way for the main course – the entrée (which needs its accent) is now the first course in France and most of the rest of the world. But in the US and Americanised parts of Britain it is, perversely, the main course. To be clear, use first or main course.

envelop, envelope

envelop is the verb, envelope the noun.

envisage, envision

although they look similar and overlap in meaning, these words are quite different in origin. Envisage is from the French *envisager*, meaning to look in the face (visage); envision is from vision, what is seen. Envisage is common in Britain; envision in the US.

Envisage is often used in British English to mean foresee or plan:

> The council envisage a time when overcrowding will be worse.

> The council envisage a time when building a block of flats will be necessary.

> The council envisage building a block of flats.

This usage is criticised as officialese by Partridge; it blurs the distinction between conceiving something as a future possibility, considering that action is necessary and deciding to act. Unless you intend to blur or mislead, avoid envisage.

Envision is used in the US as an alternative to envisage:

> An extensive 'post-occupation strategy' that envisioned an American takeover of the capital and an eventual return to power by Saddam's regime.
>
> (*International Herald Tribune*)

Exactly the same objection applies here: does envision mean nothing more than foresee or does it mean plan?

American writers also use envision to mean imagine or picture:

> She tried to envision the list on the ceiling above her bed.

> She envisioned dragging her stomach like a watermelon from table to sink.
>
> (both by Anne Tyler)

Salman Rushdie, who now lives in New York, has adopted this usage:

He envisioned wallpaper and soft furnishings, dreamed bed-sheets, designed bathroom fixtures.

To sound American use envision; otherwise use imagine or picture.

envy
is directed at a person not an attribute: 'I envy him.'
    If the envy is specific, there are two objects: 'I envy him his command of English.'

'Him' should also have been included in the following reference to Frederic Raphael by Arnold Wesker: 'I envy his classical education.'

envy, jealousy
envy refers to something we haven't got and would like to have; jealousy to something we have and want to keep for ourselves.

eponymous/ly
literary words referring to the process of deriving a name for something from (eg) a person, usually clumsy and often redundant:

> What of the man who gave his name eponymously to this massive Parisian facelift, Baron Haussmann?
>
> *(London Review of Books)*

> Guinness Cameroon, a local subsidiary of the multinational that makes the eponymous velvety black beer.
>
> *(Economist)*

equable, equitable
equable is even-tempered; equitable is fair, just.

equally as
is always wrong. Instead it should be either:

> The two of them were equally good.

or:

> She was as good as he was.

erroneous

means mistaken, containing errors:

> I consider his views erroneous.

It should not be used to refer to people as a variation on error-prone:

> A poor decision by the erroneous Russell Tiffin.
>
> (BBC online)

erstwhile

is literary for former:

> His erstwhile colleagues.

eschew

is literary for avoid, shun:

> A voracious reader, he nevertheless eschewed books on the subject.
>
> (Adam Nossiter)

especially, specially

mean the same thing but especially is formal, specially informal.

estimated at about

is always wrong: it should be either:

> The crowd was estimated at 3,500.

or :

> About 3,500 people were there.

etc

which is short for the Latin *et cetera* meaning 'and the rest', does not need a full stop after it.

ethnic minority *see* **minority ethnic**

euphemism

is a common feature of language, enabling us to avoid being explicit when the situation demands. Short direct words like sex, death, shit and piss can be translated in all sorts of ways: to sleep with and to be intimate with; to pass away and to expire; to use the lavatory, loo, toilet, bathroom, restroom, comfort station or to wash your hands, powder your nose, relieve yourself.

Rhyming slang like raspberry for fart (see **rhyming slang**) provides some colourful examples of euphemism.

War brings out the worst in our political leaders and their spin doctors who use phrases like 'collateral damage' for civilian casualties of bombing raids. This kind of language is never justified.

There are various euphemisms for sacking workers, such as downsizing, restructuring and letting people go.

euphuism

is affected, bombastic literary style.

evince

(show) is confused with evoke (draw out):

> Archer hopes that by associating himself with this great and tragic writer he will evince sympathy from readers.
>
> (*Observer*)

evocative

is a meaningless adjective when used without explanation (a thrillingly evocative novel).

evoke

is confused with **evince** and with **invoke** (call upon).

exalt, exult

to exalt is to praise; to exult to boast.

exception proves the rule

this is one of those silly phrases that people go on using because they don't think about what they're saying. How could the making of an exception to a rule validate rather than weakening it? It's obvious nonsense:

> Can you name three living British philosophers? Yes, there's Roger Scruton but he is the exception that proves the rule.
> (*Guardian*)

> Ireland was the exception that proved the rule – indeed the exception that largely wrote the rule, since that country's extraordinary relationship to the potato consolidated its dubious identity in the English mind.
> (Michael Pollan)

> He was mentioned as an indispensable contact, an exception who somehow proved the rule.
> (Adam Nossiter)

An exception can 'prove a rule' in the old sense of prove as test: the exception would test the rule, as in the proof of the pudding is in the eating. But if the exception held, it would be a breach of the rule.

Also, in law and other forms of regulation, the making of an exception suggests that a rule holds in cases not excepted. 'Smoking permitted in this room' is evidence of a general ban.

excoriate *see* **coruscate**

executor, executioner
an executor deals with a dead man's will and estate; an executioner kills him.

exert
is confused with exhibit:

> Early in his career he exerts such arrogance.
> (*Sunday Times* reader's letter)

exhibit
in British English an exhibition consists of individual exhibits; in American English the part stands for the whole:

An exhibit of his pictures at a women's club.
(Saul Bellow)

exigent, exiguous
exigent is urgent, exacting; exiguous is scanty, slender.

ex-patriot
which would mean someone who had stopped loving their country, is confused with expatriate, someone living abroad:

One English ex-patriot in Tokyo, perhaps a little the worse for Asahi lager, said he would gladly hand over the keys to his house to whoever could stop the clock right now.
(*Guardian*)

According to *Corrections and Clarifications*, the anthology of mistakes published by the *Guardian*, this is a contender for the most common one of all.

exponential
is literary for increasingly rapid or steep:

The exponential increase in private fortunes.
(*London Review of Books*)

In recent years its growth has been exponential, with total income more than tripling in the past five years.
(*Australian*)

extrovert
not extravert

exult *see* exalt, exult

eyeglasses
American for spectacles, glasses:

He had eyeglasses for nearsightedness.
(Tom Wolfe)

F

facade
does not need an accent.

famous
is almost always a redundant word: if something really is famous, we don't need to be told. The same goes for famously.

farther, farthest
use further, furthest. The distinction between farther for literal distance and further for abstract senses was never generally accepted and is dying out. *ODWE* recommends further, furthest.

fatal, mortal *see* fatality, mortality

fatality, mortality
both these words mean death, and death is usually the better word. Writing 'There were four fatalities' means no more than 'There were four deaths'. Mortality, uncommon in general usage, is the term used in medicine: 'Smallpox has a 30 per cent mortality', that is death rate. To discuss cases that did not go according to plan doctors hold 'Morbidity and mortality meetings', though the terminology adds nothing to what they are: complication and death meetings.

The distinction between fatal and mortal is more subtle. A fatal illness is one that causes death; a mortal illness is the same but with overtones of suffering. Mortal also implies that death is inevitable. People sometimes recover from 'fatal' illnesses (a disease can be usually fatal) but a mortal illness is the final illness. Mortal is not really a medical term but one with literary and religious overtones: we are mortal, ie doomed to die.

faze *see* **phase**

fed up with
something not of it; also fed up to:

> I'm fed up to the back teeth with your behaviour.

feminine forms
words ending in −ess are much less common than they were. Jewess and Negress are considered offensive and should not be used. A woman writer might be an author or a poet, but never nowadays an authoress or a poetess. A woman teacher is no longer a schoolmistress; air hostesses and stewardesses have become flight attendants; women running things are managers not manageresses.

There is feminist pressure to extend this process to words like actress and waitress (women as well as men to be actors; waiter/waitress to be replaced by something like waitperson or waitron). But the terms actress and waitress are still current: they will offend few people and confuse nobody.

Some −ess words, eg lioness for the female of the species, and the female titles (baroness, countess, duchess) are not controversial. See the Longman guide for more examples of feminine forms.

fete
doesn't need the accent.

fetid
not foetid

fettle
means set in order, arrange, hence in fine fettle.

fetus
not foetus. Although foetus is the traditional spelling in British English, medical writers in particular use the more logical fetus (the word comes from the Latin *fetus*, offspring). *ODWE* now recommends fetus and the Longman guide says: 'This is the

usual spelling in American English, and increasingly in British English, too.'

few, little
there is some confusion between few and little. It's true that few people are tempted to write 'little' (not much) instead of 'few' (not many) – 'little people' would suggest dwarfs. But the reverse mistake does crop up:

> For this she receives few thanks.
> (*Guardian*)

This should be 'little thanks'. Although 'many thanks' survives as an idiom alongside 'thanks very much', thanks is essentially a plural noun: there is nowadays no singular 'thank'. So you can't have 'few thanks', although you can have 'few thank-yous' because a thank-you is a specific event, a countable item.

Few is also out of place when things like time, distance and money are measured:

> He believed that as few as six months would suffice for this.
> (Jonathan Frantzen)

Little should be used instead of few here because 'six months' is a period of time: the months are not seen as separate entities. By contrast, you could say that few months are shorter than 31 days.

fewer, less
the traditional distinction between fewer and less is still going strong: fewer is used of number and less of quantity so you have fewer trees and less wood. Thus at a supermarket checkout the fast lane should advertise itself as for 'fewer than 10 items' not for 'less than 10 items' because what counts is the number of items not the weight or bulk of the goods or how much money they cost.

Some literate shoppers have forced supermarkets to change from less to fewer – which shows that the distinction is by no means obsolete. And when the *Times* pundit Philip Howard criticised 'Notting Hill pedants' for doing just this, a reader's letter put him right: 'Useful distinctions between "less" and "fewer" can and should be made. Is there not a world of difference between an editor asking his columnists to write fewer pedantic articles and asking them to write less pedantic articles?'

Above all, less should not be used of people:

> There were never less than 30 or 40 people a day needing help.
>
> (Doris Lessing)

> Having had in his house no less than five Nobel Prize winners.
>
> (Margaret Drabble)

> The police surgeon, and no less than three outside doctors, confirmed the opinion.
>
> (Iris Murdoch)

The last two examples are quoted by Burchfield who refuses to criticise them – but I think he is wrong. In each case fewer should replace less because people are countable. Indeed in these examples they are actually counted.

On the other hand, measurements of time, distance and money all take less not fewer: less than two hours, less than two miles, less than £2. And in the measurement of reading and writing, too, less is used instead of fewer. I read less than 200 pages a day and write less than 2,000 words a day. The reason here is that numbers give the size of a quantity.

So the following are mistakes:

> In return for a plea to attempted manslaughter he served fewer than two years.
>
> (*Guardian*)

> When Larkin died, his reputation rested on three books of poems, each of fewer than 50 pages.
>
> (Blake Morrison)

In each case less should replace fewer.

There are borderline cases where less is used instead of fewer because the sense is more quantity or extent than number. Longman quotes Alan Sillitoe: 'Emerging from the melee with less wounds than his brothers.' And Burchfield quotes the *Listener*: 'A traffic expert who believes in building less roads, not more.' In these examples less sounds wrong because it comes before a countable plural and fewer would not be an improvement because of the sense. They are better rewritten: 'less badly wounded' and 'less, not more, road-building'.

A similar point applies to sport where points or goals or runs are both countable and seen as measurement. In the following examples fewer has been used where less would also be possible:

> He must be confident that his bowlers can dismiss the opposition for fewer than 300.
>
> (*Observer*)

> Victory by many fewer than 30 points would indicate a poor return for England.
>
> (*Times*)

Note that here, because a target is specified, a round figure is quoted – 300 not 303, 30 not 33 – which strengthens the argument for less. But it is difficult to say that either less or fewer is wrong.

And what about percentages? If a minority of people support the government, are they fewer or less than 50 per cent? Nowadays the population and the electorate are usually given a plural verb: 'The population have ...' 'The electorate are ...' This strengthens the case for fewer:

> Fewer than 25 per cent of the electorate support the war.

Then there are words like groceries and clothes that are essentially plurals: you can't have fewer groceries or clothes. So the following are mistakes:

> Money would run out earlier and either the gas meter would not be fed or fewer groceries would be collected.
>
> (Roy Hattersley)

> The female dancers wore substantially fewer clothes than the men.
>
> (*Times*)

In these cases the solution to the problem is not to replace fewer by less: less groceries and less clothes both sound wrong. Instead, try 'less food would be collected' and 'wore substantially less'.

Finally, it's always one less rather than one fewer. William Safire of the *New York Times*, who is perhaps the best-known commentator on language in the US, was corrected by a reader for writing:

> That was one fewer career lost to the predatory polygraph.

He acknowledged his mistake – a breach of idiom rather than grammar.

fiancé, fiancée
need their accents.

figures
figures under 10 are usually written out in words: one, two, three ... with numbers starting at 10; where nine and 10 crop up together it's usually 9–10. See **numbers**.

film noir
not noire

fine-tooth comb
not fine-toothed comb or fine toothcomb/tooth-comb. Most experts recommend fine-tooth comb (a comb with fine teeth), whereas Kingsley Amis (quoted by Lynne Truss) claims that it was once possible to buy something called a toothcomb; 'a fine toothcomb' therefore would have been one with particularly fine teeth. In his favour is the undoubted fact that we pronounce 'tooth comb' as though the two words were one. But, in punctuating, why bother your reader with this? Stick to fine-tooth comb, which is both logical and generally accepted.

first
can be redundant:

> I have been credited with first introducing him [Mick Jagger] to Tony Blair.
>
> (Robert Harris)

first, second, third

not firstly, secondly, thirdly:

> I want to make two points: first, be brief; second, be accurate.

first and second

confusion rules:

> Sir Richard Eyre will direct *Atonement* – his second film
> venture since adapting and directing the story of the novelist
> Iris Murdoch.
>
> (*Guardian*)

No: his first. It would be his second only if the sentence stopped after
venture.

first name

has replaced forename and is replacing Christian name.

first world war *see* world war

flaccid

is literary for limp:

> Batting was never going to be a cinch. But some of the
> dismissals were flaccid.
>
> (*Guardian*)

flammable, inflammable

both these words mean easily set on fire. Flammable is now preferred
by fire-prevention experts because it is unambiguous. The negative
form is non-flammable.

flaunt

(show off) is confused with flout (treat with contempt):

> They [the French] are also ardent individualists, proud of
> flaunting the law.
>
> (*Observer*)

fledgling
not fledgeling

floating participle *see* **dangling modifiers**

flout *see* **flaunt**

focused, focusing
not focussed, focussing

folie à deux
a delusion jointly held by two people.

folk
is already a plural for people in general but an s is often added, as with my folks (parents) and old folks' home.

following
is journalese for after:

> In 1970 she [Myrella Cohen] took silk, only the second Jewish woman to do so following Rose Heilbron.
>
> *(Times)*

Also, as with **first and second**, it should be either 'the second Jewish woman to do so' full stop or 'the first Jewish woman to do so after Rose Heilbron'.

forbear
(to refrain) is different from forebear (ancestor).

forceful, forcible
there is a traditional distinction between these similar-sounding adjectives and their adverbs forcefully and forcibly. Forcible/y is used to emphasise that an action is one of physical force, as in forcible entry and:

> Mr Armey said he did not believe 'peaceful Palestinian civilians should be forcibly expelled'.
>
> *(Guardian)*

If the idea of physical force is already contained in the sentence, forcible would be redundant but forceful suggests that the attack will be powerful:

> Israel's prime minister, Ariel Sharon, was last night poised to order a forceful military assault on the Palestinians.
>
> (*Guardian*)

But forcibly has become the fashionable way of saying 'in a forceful manner':

> What struck Fay most forcibly was the fact that he looked exactly as he always did.
>
> (Carol Shields)

> The simplicity and truth of this notion struck him so forcibly.
>
> (Elizabeth Jane Howard)

> She had forcibly channelled all her wanting into the numbered days that the luxury cruise would last.
>
> (Jonathan Frantzen)

> A man will step over a bursting rubbish bag until it is squirming with maggots unless forcibly told to remove it.
>
> (*Sunday Times*)

On the basis of the traditional distinction 'forcibly told' in the last example would presumably be by means of a rolling-pin. But to most writers and readers the distinction is lost.

forego

(go before) is different from forgo (do without).

foreign words

be careful with foreign words and phrases. Don't overuse them unless you want to parade your knowledge of foreign languages. And try to ensure that your reader will understand what you're saying. In general, if a word needs italics because it is unfamiliar, it should be translated into English.

forensic

is loosely used. In the scientific sense, it is not a specific method but describes the use of science or technology in the investigation and establishment of facts or evidence in a court of law.

forever

is now usually one word.

format, formatted, formatting

are the accepted spellings.

former

means once (a former footballer) and also the first-named person in a sentence as opposed to the second-named person, the latter. This is a clumsy and oldfashioned construction and should be avoided; it's far better to repeat the names:

> John and Henry are both footballers. John is a striker and Henry a defender.

formerly

is confused with formally:

> She wrote to the company to formerly cancel the order.

formulas

is the ordinary plural of formula, though mathematicians and chemists continue to use formulae.

forte

strength, does not have an accent, though it is pronounced 'fortay'.

fortuitous

the traditional meaning is accidental – something that happens by chance – but it is often used as a near-synonym of fortunate. It is particularly used when an event is seen as both accidental and fortunate. But to be clear, prefer fortunate, lucky or propitious.

four-letter words

there are more four-letter (and other swear) words in public writing – books, plays, newspapers, TV and radio – than ever before, though some publications still use asterisks to spare their readers the sight of the actual word. In Britain the *Guardian* has led the way on the use of fuck, at times adopting an almost missionary position. For example, it published a feature in 2002 in which a variety of trendy people (including a professor of English) lined up to say that fuck wasn't really a shocking word any more. One woman neatly combined trendiness and snobbery by saying: 'I'd rather my children said fuck than toilet.'

Not long afterwards, in January 2003, the *Guardian* came seriously unstuck with its Cilla Black issue. The problem was a cover, designed for the tabloid section by the artist Gillian Wearing, which featured the words 'FUCK CILLA BLACK'. Reader reaction was, according to the readers' editor Ian Mayes, unprecedented. Even the paper's staff voted 140 to 88 that the decision to publish the cover was wrong.

By coincidence the next day's *Evening Standard* included a TV review by Victor Lewis-Smith which opened with a short lecture on the grammatical possibilities of the word fuck – or as the *Standard* had it, f**k. A sample: 'In its classic usage it's an abstract noun (he really gives a f**k) but it also functions as an adverbial intensifier (she is f**king interested in him) and is equally useful as an interjection (f**k, I'm late for class).'

It's clear that while some people are offended by the F word, others now aren't. Many more people are offended by the C word.

Soon after the *Guardian* incident the Brisbane press reported that a young motorcyclist had pleaded guilty to 'exhibiting an indecent publication' after being stopped by police while wearing a T-shirt with the slogan 'Jesus is a cunt'. The Australian Council of Civil Liberties commented that there were limits to freedom of speech; the F word would still be considered offensive if used in the wrong place, such as a church, and the C word was seen as deeply offensive.

In the same month the Australian cricketer Darren Lehmann received a five-match ban for calling the Sri Lankans 'black cunts'. His offence was not the abusive and sexist C word but 'racism', ie the word black – see **black**. It was clear that the C word was pretty routine in the exchange of insults that modern international cricketers call sledging.

If there is a general lesson to be drawn from these examples it is that four-letter words apparently accepted in one context can be deeply offensive in another. Use them with great care.

Frankenstein

was not the monster but the scientist (in Mary Shelley's novel *Frankenstein*) who made the monster.

free gift

a particularly silly example of tautology - what would an unfree gift be?

freelance

not freelancer – though the American form is increasingly common:

> A *Time* magazine freelancer and *Sunday Times* stringer.
> <div align="right">(<i>Guardian</i>)</div>

French

ever since the Norman conquest, the French language has enjoyed high cultural prestige and a powerful influence. Today it is, for example, the language of food, fashion, film, fornication and formality.

We eat an omelette or a pâté, wear culottes and a brassière or bra (though French people call it a soutien-gorge), watch a film noir made by an auteur. And we make love (or have sex) in French as well – from a French kiss by way of a French (oral sex) to a French letter. The late Alex Comfort's book *The Joy of Sex* is full of French terms like *cassolette, pattes d'arraignée, la petite mort*. As an American reviewer said of it, the book is 'basically a Larousse Erotique'.

Which is all very well. The problem is that we are inclined to find French naughtiness everywhere. It's the ooh-la-la effect. So the plain word for a paunch, **embonpoint**, gets twisted to mean large breasts. And the word for the state of being partly dressed, **déshabillé**, becomes a superior way of saying nudity. Or how about this from the *Sunday Times*?

> The news from France took a welcome deviation from politics last week to a story with a distinctly ooh-la-la flavour. It seems somehow appropriate that although she apparently operated all over Europe, Margaret MacDonald should have been arrested for running an upmarket prostitution agency in Paris, spiritual home of la grande horizontale.

Finally, when we want to be formal, we relapse into French. We ask the people we invite to RSVP (*répondez s'il vous plaît*). And we put on all sorts of airs and graces: we say things like actualité instead of truth, commence instead of begin, reticent instead of reluctant – and our English suffers as a result.

fulsome

can be used both positively (abundant, full) and negatively (over-abundant, excessive). Both the *Observer* and the *Guardian* plead guilty to misusing the word; that is they admit using it in a positive sense when their style guides define it as excessive or insincere. But – to show how difficult it is to maintain this policy – *Guardian* readers' editor Ian Mayes himself writes:

> On at least two occasions we have run immediate and fulsome apologies.
>
> (*Corrections and Clarifications*)

According to Kate Burridge the earliest recorded sense of fulsome (from the thirteenth century) is positive (abundant, full, good) but gradually the negative senses became dominant. She says that in 1868 someone used the expression 'this fulsome world' following it with a note 'I use the word fulsome in the original sense' – meaning abundantly good. Writers and editors then couldn't stop the meaning of fulsome shifting towards 'excessive, offensive', just as writers and editors today can't stop the meaning from shifting back.

Whatever the style guides recommend, fulsome is now more often used in a positive sense:

> A friend congratulated me in fulsome terms.
>
> (American language expert Geoffrey Nunberg)

> They were fulsome in their praise for her garden./When Alice remonstrated with Tony she was fulsome in his praise.
>
> (Margaret Forster)

And so is the clumsy adverb fulsomely:

> I thanked Mr Boateng fulsomely.
>
> (Roy Kerridge, writing in the *Spectator*, reprinted by the *Sunday Times*)

But whatever you intend to say when you use fulsome, you risk being misunderstood.

furore
not furor

further, furthest *see* **farther, farthest**

G

gaff, gaffe
use gaff for the hook to land a fish and for blow the gaff (disclose a secret); a gaffe is a blunder.

gambit
a gambit is an opening move in chess which sacrifices a piece to gain a subsequent advantage, so 'opening' before gambit is redundant. But since most non-chess players don't recognise gambit as an opening move, the word is best avoided.

gamble, gambol
two kinds of play. To gamble is to risk money in a game of chance or to bet on anything; to gambol is to frisk like a spring lamb.

gaol
use jail.

gases
not gasses

gateau
in English does not need a circumflex accent.

gay
once meant lively with a suggestion of loose living: a gay bachelor was an enthusiastic heterosexual. Now gay almost always means homo-sexual. But not always:

> Simone Deflandre, a gay divorcee in her early thirties who had
> been a nurse and masseuse, ran the Bar de la Plage and went
> out with Captain Piel.
>
> > (Robert Gildea)

> Take a Chance on Me. Black profess F 50, loves fun and gay
> times ...
>
> > (Women seeking men, *Observer*, 22 December 2002)

Gay can also be used to mean silly, affected:

> If AA Gill can't see the difference between the magnificent
> Sophie Dahl and the minging Meg Matthews, then he's even
> gayer than I thought.
>
> > (*Sunday Times* letter from Julie Burchill)

Advice: to avoid being misunderstood, use gay only to mean
homosexual.

geezer, geyser
a geezer is informal for an odd old man or – in London English – a
man. A geyser is a hot spring or a bathroom water heater.

gendarmes
in France are technically not police officers. The Gendarmerie
Nationale, which is responsible for policing small towns and the
countryside, is distinct from the French police force and is a branch of
the army.

gender
traditionally refers to masculine, feminine and (where appropriate)
neuter in language. It is also the trendy word for the differences
between men and women:

> The General Synod (of the Scottish Episcopal Church) is to
> vote on a proposal to remove from canon law all references to
> gender in criteria for the episcopate.
>
> > (*Times*)

This leads to clumsy, pompous phrases like 'a person of the female gender'. But having separate words for sexual activity (sex) and sexual difference (gender) can be useful:

> Even when sex was invented, it initially lacked gender. There were no males and females.
>
> *(Sunday Times)*

Many good writers will continue to use 'sex' for both activity and difference. Other people insist on using 'gender' for both:

> We now frequently spend time together, but the relationship has plateaued at a pleasant but apparently gender-free level. We seem to avoid physical contact and have never even kissed.
>
> (Private lives letter, *Guardian*)

Language expert and feminist Deborah Cameron has complained about 'the way many English-speakers now use gender as a polite synonym for sex: you hear people inquiring about the gender of animals'. She says that for the feminists who 'did most to put the word into circulation, gender was a technical term which took its meaning from a contrast with sex'. The intended contrast was between the biological (sex) and the social (gender), which was related to the feminist claim that many traditional differences between men and women were social rather than biological in origin. This distinction between 'sex' and 'gender' is not generally recognised.

Advice: if you want to be trendy, use gender for the differences (whether biological or social) between men and women; otherwise use sex. Use sex for animals (and for human sexual activity).

genetic *see* **congenital, genetic/hereditary**

genocide
like obscene, is overused as a term of severe disapproval. It means the deliberate extermination of a race or people rather than mass killing. So this reference to the Balkans and Rwanda is over the top:

> We have stood indifferently by while several genocides happened..
>
> (John Lloyd of the *New Statesman* writing in the *Evening Standard*)

Extending the word to cover culture is, if anything, worse, as in this reference to Welsh:

> A language once spoken by a whole people – and then picked off by cultural genocide.
>
> (Hywel Williams)

What is implied here is that imposing a language on people who speak another is comparable to mass killing, which is ridiculous.

Extending the word to cover animals is the ultimate absurdity, as in a reference by a Tory MP to the Blair government's 'mass genocide' of hounds because of its decision to ban hunting.

genteelism

is a particular form of euphemism: a perfectly good plain word like sweat is seen as vulgar and replaced by perspire. Other examples are bosom for breast(s), expectorate for spit, odour for smell and soil for dirty. Toilet, which used to be a genteelism for lavatory, is now generally accepted.

geriatric

is the adjective from geriatrics, medical care of old people. It is also a popular term of abuse for football referees, cricket umpires and judges. If the word offends, it is intended to.

germane

is literary for relevant, appropriate:

> Such reflections had become germane.
> (Salman Rushdie)

gerund

a term from Latin used to describe a verb-noun ending in –ing (as opposed to a present participle):

> Smoking is bad for you. (gerund)

> He was smoking./He came in smoking. (participle)

The main problem with the gerund occurs when it is used with another noun or a pronoun in a possessive sense: 'I object to John/him smoking' is the common form while 'I object to John's/his smoking' is traditionally considered correct. But it would be pedantic to write:

I don't object to anybody's smoking.

The common form is fine unless the 'correct' form is essential for clarity. There is a distinction between John smoking on a particular occasion or in a particular place and his smoking habit:

I don't object to John smoking in the sitting-room this evening.

I don't object to John's smoking or his drinking; it's his anecdotes I can't stand.

Trask distinguishes between the verbal noun in 'The *smoking* of cigarettes is forbidden' and the gerund in '*Smoking* cigarettes is forbidden'. He explains that the verbal noun functions in every way as a noun, eg it is followed by 'of', while the gerund keeps its verbal properties, eg it can be followed by an object. Unfortunately, he then insists on the use of the possessive 's for the gerund as well as the verbal noun, telling readers who find the possessive form unnatural to grit their teeth and learn it.

Somehow I can't see him having much success.

get
there is nothing wrong with this powerful short word but its effect can be dulled by repetition. See **gotten**.

ghettos
not ghettoes

gibe, gybe, jibe
to gibe is to sneer; to gybe is a nautical term meaning to change course; jibe (with) is American for agree, be in accord.

gift
is a noun. But the verb to gift has been used about members of the royal family giving servants presents of official gifts to sell for themselves.

gild, guild
to gild is cover with gold; a guild is an association.

gilt, guilt
gilt is covered with gold; guilt is responsibility for wrongdoing.

gipsy *see* **gypsy**

goodbye
is one word.

goodwill
is one word.

gotten
is American but no longer British English (except in the phrase 'ill-gotten gains').

gourmand, gourmet
both refer to the enjoyment of food; a gourmand is inclined to be greedy, a gourmet discriminating.

graceful, gracious
both these words come from grace. Graceful usually refers to physical movement though it can also mean behaving well; gracious usually refers to superior people behaving well towards their inferiors – being condescending. The Queen is characteristically gracious, and gracious living suggests the upper classes setting a good stylistic example.

graffiti
is the plural of graffito. Try to use graffiti, because it is more familiar, followed by a plural verb – unless, of course, you wish to parade your knowledge of Italian.

grandad
but granddaughter

grands prix
is the plural of grand prix (motor racing).

grey
not gray, which is American

grievous
not grievious

grill, grille
to grill is to cook by radiant heat (under a grill) or to interrogate; a grille is a grating.

grisly, gristly, grizzly
grisly is causing terror; gristly (of meat) is full of gristle; grizzly is grey-haired or grey-bearded and the name given to the large American bear.

groin, groyne
the groin is the join between abdomen and thigh; a groyne is a beach breakwater to prevent erosion.

grottoes
not grottos

ground rules
in Britain the ground rules are usually the basic principles or rules of procedure (from ground meaning bottom). Both Chambers and Oxford give this definition for ground rule, though Chambers adds a second, contradictory one: 'a modifying (sports) rule for a particular place or circumstance'.

Cochrane prefers this second definition ('Correctly, the special *rules* pertaining to a particular playing-*ground*, course or court') and Trask insists that in both cricket and baseball 'the ground rules are the special rules introduced to deal with the features of individual playing grounds'. He may be right about baseball but he is certainly wrong about cricket, which does not use this expression: cricket has laws not rules (though it does have supplementary 'regulations').

To ensure clarity, don't use ground rules. Instead use either basic/fundamental rules or local rules, which is a golf term for the regulations governing individual courses.

Gulf War syndrome *see* syndrome

guru

a (Hindu) spiritual teacher, is often misused to mean any old expert:

> Follow the travel gurus to find your perfect holiday.
> (*Sunday Times*)

gypsy

not gipsy. A Gypsy is a member of the Romany people. As an adjective gypsy suggests a relaxed, outdoor and bohemian way of life.

H

habit
a habit is customary behaviour so usual before habit is redundant.

hale, hail
hale is healthy, hence hale and hearty; to hail is to greet or salute, hence hail-fellow-well-met; to hail from is to come from; hail is frozen rain.

hallo *see* **hello**

handkerchiefs
not handkerchieves

hangar, hanger
a hangar is an aircraft shed; a hanger is for clothes.

hanged, hung
people are (or used to be) hanged; pictures and pheasants are hung.

hanging participles *see* **dangling modifiers**

harass, harassment
have only one r.

harbinger
is literary for sign, usually a bad one:

The bird seems to be a harbinger of a harrowing mental breakdown.

(Guardian)

Used as a verb, the word is even more literary, even archaic:

> To rip out the mainspring of a free society ... cannot but harbinger ill for our country.
> (Frank Field, Daily Telegraph)

A plain word like threaten would be better here.

harebrained
not hare-brained, hairbrained

hat–trick
not hattrick or hat trick

haven
a haven is a harbour and so a place of refuge; safe before haven is redundant.

having said that
is a longwinded way of saying but.

he/she, s/he, he or she
are clumsy, pedantic and unnecessary formulas since 'they' stands idiomatically and correctly for the singular of both sexes. (In the same way 'them' does for him/her, 'their' for his/her and 'theirs' for his/hers.) The only sensible reason for using 'he or she' instead of 'they' would be to emphasise that the reference is to both men and women. So in almost all cases 'he or she' should be 'they':

> If somebody calls, they [not 'he or she'] can expect a drink.

The argument is stronger when the pronoun has to be repeated: a second or third 'he or she' makes the sentence even more clumsy:

If somebody calls, he or she can expect a drink if he or she is thirsty etc.

To avoid the problem of repetition some writers follow 'he or she' by 'they':

Why when a successful executive has more money than he or she will ever spend, do they submit themselves to 12-hour days?

(*Guardian*)

Others follow 'he or she' by 'he'. The novelist and biographer DJ Taylor starts off referring to the average biographer as 'he or she' but continues:

However hard he labours, however many people he interviews, however strenuous his wrestling with the facts …

It's far simpler to use 'they' throughout.

To avoid being clumsy and sexist some writers now alternate between 'he' and 'she' (instead of 'they') in successive paragraphs or sections. This is an irritating and distracting device which raises the question: is there any reason why a particular paragraph or section should attract the masculine or the feminine pronoun?

But above all it is unnecessary. As Burchfield says:

Over the centuries writers of standing have used they, their and them with reference to a singular pronoun or noun, and the practice has continued in the 20th century to the point that, traditional grammarians aside, such constructions are hardly noticed any more.

And we are now in the 21st century.

head up
means head: drop the up.

heeled

means shod, hence well-heeled for affluent; but better-heeled doesn't work.

heft

is American for weight, heaviness, solidity:

> Go ahead, pick it up. The heft tells you it's solid sterling silver.
> (*Scientific American* quoted by Oxford)

> The sheer existential heft of a tomato or cucumber.
> (Michael Pollan)

> A cot was too small for a man of his heft.
> (Gloria Emerson)

In British usage the verb to heft is to lift or weigh, and hefty (for heavily built) is common.

heist

is a trendy word for armed robbery; it comes from the US and is here to stay.

hello

not hallo, hullo

hereditary *see* **congenital**

heroin, heroine

heroin (the drug) and heroine (female hero) are occasionally confused by the most unlikely people. FW Hodgson in his book *New Subediting* quotes without comment:

> Teenage runaway Kirsty McFadden has revealed how she earned an astonishing £600 a week begging on the streets of Bristol to feed her heroine habit.
> (Bristol *Evening Post*)

hew, hue
to hew is to chop with heavy blows; a hue is a colour or shade of colour and also a clamour; hence hue-and-cry.

hiccup
not hiccough

hierarchy
not heirarchy

high jinks
not hi-jinx

hijack
not highjack

hike
is journalese for increase as both noun and verb:

> House prices could rise by more than 30 per cent before slowing down in response to expected interest-rate hikes.

> Brown's decision to hike government borrowing.
> *(Sunday Times)*

him/her *see* **he/she, s/he, he or she**

hippy
not hippie

his/her *see* **he/she, s/he, he or she**

historic, historical
historic is important in history; historical is to do with history. So a historic event stands out; a historical event occurred in history as opposed to myth. But Chambers points out that historic and historical were once used interchangeably. And there are two current uses of

historic where you would expect historical: historic tenses in grammar are narrative tenses; historic cost in accountancy is the original cost of an item as opposed to the cost of replacing it. *See also*: **a/an**.

hi-tech
not high-tech or hi-tec

hoard, horde
a hoard is a hidden supply; a horde is a tribe or crowd.

Hobson's choice
is no choice at all, not a difficult one.

hoi polloi
from the Greek, is a derogatory term for the common people. Because *hoi* means the, it's technically incorrect to refer to 'the hoi polloi', but this is a 'mistake' sanctioned by usage.

holey, holy
holey is full of holes; holy is saintly, religious.

holocaust
from the Greek *kanatos* (burnt), means huge slaughter, particularly by fire. *The* Holocaust is the mass murder of the Jews and others by the Nazis. This is a powerful, emotive word to be used with care. The firestorm bombing of German cities like Dresden and Hamburg could reasonably be described as a holocaust:

> The holocaust being inflicted on the cities of the Reich.
> (Robert Gildea)

But this reference to Salman Rushdie's fatwa and 9/11 is forced:

> That solitary hell through which Rushdie lived has perhaps been burned out of popular memory by the vastly greater holocaust of 2001.
> (Hugo Young, *Observer*)

homely

in American refers to looks and means ugly; homely in British refers to character and means friendly, kindly.

> Patch had been a downright homely child, a spiky, knobby, wiry child, quarrelsome and thorny.
>
> (Anne Tyler)

> In contrast with Heather, with whom I never had any real peace of mind, my wife is honest and homely.
>
> (*Sunday Times*)

There are clear signs of the American usage coming to Britain:

> A woman so homely that, when she was born, her mother saw the afterbirth and shouted 'It's twins.'
>
> (Victor Lewis-Smith, *Evening Standard*)

But which is this?

> Imagine, if you will, a homely kind of girl – well-liked but usually ignored – who lives next door to the town hunk.
>
> (Matthew Engel, a British journalist, in the *Guardian* about the relations between Canada and the US)

Use this word with care to avoid confusion and offence.

homey

not homy for homelike

homogeneous, homogenous

the first, in general use, means consistent, uniform; the second is a biological term meaning similar because of common descent.

homonym, homophone

both refer to two or more similar words that are different in meaning. Homonyms are spelt (and usually pronounced) alike: bail (security) and bail (barrier) are homonyms. Homophones are pronounced alike but spelt differently: bail (security) and bale (evil) are homophones.

In writing it is homophones that cause most of the trouble, as is shown by common confusions like complement/compliment, formally/formerly, hoard/horde, phase/faze, pore/pour etc.

homosexual
there is confusion between *homos* (Greek, the same) and *homo* (Latin, man). Homosexual comes from *homos* and means same sex; it refers to both men and women.

hooray *see* hurray

hopefully
there is no sound grammatical objection to the use of hopefully to mean 'it is hoped' – see **dangling modifiers**. But there are several reasons why you should pause before using hopefully in this way.

First, this usage is bound to upset some people. Does this matter to you? Might this interfere with your message?

Second, the usage is inherently vague: 'Hopefully he will not do it again' shows that the speaker/writer holds this opinion but not who else holds it. As Bryson says: 'All too often the word is used as no more than an easy escape from having to take responsibility for a sentiment and as such is to be deplored.' So do you want to be vague?

Third, ambiguity is possible: 'He will go hopefully tomorrow' could mean that he is hopeful or that I (as the writer/speaker) am.

Nothing can remove hopefully from popular speech but writers should use it with care.

hors d'oeuvre
is both singular and plural. In Europe the hors d'oeuvre is the first course; in the US hors d'oeuvre are served with drinks beforehand.

hospitalise
not hospitalize – but try to use send/admit to hospital (there is a difference) instead. Partridge calls hospitalise 'shocking officialese'.

host
is now commonly used as a verb to mean act as host.

hot chips *see* chips

housebuyer, housekeeper etc
one word

house style
(style of the house) is the way a publication or printer decides to publish in matters of detail such as −ise/−ize spellings, single or double quote marks and when to use italic type. Pointless variation is distracting: a consistent style helps the reader concentrate on what the writer is saying. The argument applies to all writers, particularly those who have a collective voice because they belong to the same organisation.

hove
comes from heave, which means lift or be lifted, retch, haul, and also move (into position or sight), originally a nautical expression. In most senses the past tense (and participle) of heave is heaved but in the nautical sense it is hove:

The ship hove into view.

But there is no verb to hove; hoved and hoves are always wrong as here:

But this week another scenario hoved into view.
(*Guardian*)

however
should be followed by a comma when it means but:

However, not everybody agrees.

But when it means 'no matter how' there is no comma:

However hard you try, you won't succeed.

hullo *see* **hello**

hummus, humus
hummus is purée of chickpeas and sesame oil; humus is rotted organic matter used by gardeners.

humorist, humorous
not humourist, humourous

hung *see* **hanged, hung**

hurray
not hurrah, hooray, except in Hooray Henry, a rich ineffectual young man

hyphens
are useful: the fad for trying to do without them is silly:

> The naked child ran out of the hide covered lean-to towards the rocky beach.
>
> (Jean M Auel)

Hide-covered would be more easily read.

Whenever possible make two hyphenated words one: change wicket-keeper to wicketkeeper but keep the hyphen in hat-trick (because of the double t). And never put a hyphen after an -ly adverb: closely knit needs no hyphen because the two words can only mean knit in a close way.

I

I/me

in traditional grammar I is the subject, me the object:

I enjoy wine./Wine pleases me.

The same distinction applies to he/him, she/her, we/us and they/them (though you does not vary in this way).

The verb to be takes a complement rather than an object, so the pronoun that follows is traditionally subjective not objective: 'It is I' is technically correct. But the common form 'It's me' is now accepted by almost everybody.

Using me instead of I as the subject of a sentence mimics some forms of popular speech:

Me and my boyfriend mooned at them out of the window.
(Zoe Williams, *Guardian*)

But this is not accepted in ordinary writing. And nor is the common error of putting I instead of me after a preposition. Except in dialect people do not say 'You live next door to I.' But many do say – and write – 'You live next door to my husband and I.' It should be 'my husband and me'. To avoid this error check by rereading what you have written without the 'my husband'.

We appears instead of us even without the equivalent of 'my husband':

I have this vision of we, the workforce.
(Fay Weldon)

A feeling of we against them.
(Doris Lessing)

The technical term favoured by we non-medics.
(*Times*)

In each case we should be us.

See also: **who/whom.**

idiosyncrasy
not idiosyncracy

ie
which is short for the Latin *id est*, meaning that is, does not need full stops or a comma after it.

ilk
which comes from old English and means same, has a specialised use in Scotland: of the same place, territorial designation or name. So 'Guthrie of that ilk' means Guthrie of Guthrie. Elsewhere it is loosely used to mean family, class, kind:

He and I – *we* could understand each other, owing to our common ilk.
(Saul Bellow)

It is often derogatory or dismissive:

The slasher movie and its blood-stained ilk.
(*Guardian*)

Use this word with care: you may annoy the purists, particularly Scottish ones, and confuse people in general.

illusion *see* **delusion, illusion**

imbed *see* **embed**

imbibe

is literary for drink.

immanent, imminent

immanent means inherent, as in this reference to the philosopher Spinoza:

> His system left no room for transcendence; his God was wholly immanent, in some sense synonymous with nature.
>
> (Jonathan Bate)

Imminent means about to happen.

imply, infer

the traditional – and useful – distinction is clear. A speaker or writer implies, ie suggests a meaning that is not explicitly stated. A listener or reader infers, ie concludes something from the words of a speaker or writer. So if you imply something, I infer it from what you say.

Because they are logically related the two words are often confused:

> Mr Byers did not take any part in the decision to suspend Mr Jones, officials said. But the clear inference was that Mr Sixsmith's No 2 may have been involved.
>
> (*Guardian*)

Here inference should be replaced by implication: the officials were implying that Jones may have been involved. But it would also be possible to insert 'to be drawn' after inference and convey essentially the same message. *See also*: **mirror words**.

impostor

not imposter

impractical, impracticable

impracticable describes plans and projects that cannot be carried out, whereas impractical is a more general word meaning not practical. An impracticable plan could also be called impractical – but so could the person who proposed it, perhaps because it was a foolish one, ie not worth carrying out even if it were practicable. Their attitude or approach would be impractical, too.

in, on

British English uses in where American uses on in common expressions like 'in/on the street' and 'in/on the team'. In London the traditional English restaurant Simpson's in the Strand is almost nextdoor to Smollensky's on the Strand, a jazz joint.

The American journalist Andrew Meldrum reported from Zimbabwe: 'Henry Olonga is no longer on the team.' Unfortunately the game was cricket and the newspaper the *Guardian*.

inadmissible

not inadmissable

inchoate

most dictionaries don't even acknowledge there is a problem with this word. Chambers, for example, defines inchoate as 'only begun; unfinished, rudimentary; not established'. It ignores the fact that inchoate is used much more often as a literary way of saying incoherent, confused, as in this reference to George W Bush:

> He was relatively inchoate until September 11. Then the American people bonded with him.
>
> (*Sunday Times*)

> Against the background of inchoate green a contrasting color by itself could well be an accident of some kind.
>
> (Michael Pollan)

> The anti-globalisation movement is constantly lambasted for its inchoate and impractically diverse demands.
>
> (*Guardian*)

Inchoate is sometimes used in the 'correct' sense to mean rudimentary, as in this reference to Elvis Presley:

He was pre-baby boom and grew up at a time when youth culture was inchoate, and almost clandestine.

(Guardian)

In some cases it's difficult to be certain which use is intended:

How wonderful it would be if children made a smooth transition from pre-teen to adulthood, without all this inchoate rebellion.

(Guardian)

Is the rebellion incoherent or rudimentary? If you care about the distinction, you'll be inclined to do without the word inchoate altogether.

incidence, prevalence
these are technical terms used in medicine to define how common a disease is. The incidence is the number of cases in general (eg 25 cases per 100,000 population per year); the prevalence is the number of cases at any one time (eg 50 cases per 100,000 population).

incidentally
not incidently

incubus
a devil supposed to have sex with women in their sleep, is over the top for severe disadvantage (nightmare would be OK):

Brian Behan often complained that his surname was something of an incubus.

(Times obituary)

indicate
is the precise word for a car driver using indicators. It is also literary for point out, show, imply, suggest, state, say etc. When it replaces point out or show it is usually clear at least:

He indicated the route they should follow.

But when it replaces imply, say etc, it is often ambiguous. In 'Officials indicated that France would not use its veto' it isn't clear whether the officials came out and said so or implied that this was likely. If you want to be vague and a bit pretentious, indicate is for you; otherwise use a clear word like imply or say.

indigene
is literary for native.

indigenous
means native-born, so non-indigenous means born in another country, not non-white.

ineluctable
is literary for inescapable.

in fact
is misused in the same way as literally:

> The aerodrome ... In fact it was a pigsty, decrepit, malodorous, with sweating walls and two-inch roaches.
> (Salman Rushdie)

In fact it wasn't a pigsty: it was an aerodrome.

infallible
means incapable of error: the Pope is said to be infallible. It is also loosely used to mean certain to happen: instead use inevitable, certain, sure-fire ...

infectious *see* **contagious, infectious**

infer *see* **imply, infer**

infinitive, split *see* **split infinitive**

inflammable *see* **flammable, inflammable**

inform

there is a literary use of inform to mean shape or inspire, as opposed to the ordinary meaning of tell:

> Emerson remains the central figure in American culture and informs our politics.
>
> (Harold Bloom)

ingenious, ingenuous

ingenious (clever) is confused with ingenuous, which is almost its opposite: artless, almost naive.

ingenue

which needs no accent, means an inexperienced, artless girl or young woman, particularly on the stage; there is a masculine form, ingenu, but it is rarely used in English. Since it is feminine, ingenue cannot be used of men as it is here by the cricket correspondent of the *Times*:

> It was a happy day for ingenues.

initials

like other abbreviations, do not need full stops.

inning, innings

in baseball a team has an inning; in cricket it is an innings. The plural of both is innings.

John Burnside in a poem called 'America' has a gaggle of children 'in some blue-lit Kansas town' playing out 'the final innings'. Although some cricket is played in the US, baseball is dominant: it's more likely to have been an inning.

innuendoes

not innuendos

inoculate

not innoculate

inoculation, vaccination

these words are now synonymous. Vaccination originally referred to the use of cowpox to protect against smallpox.

inquire/y

not enquire/y. Some sources, eg *ODWE*, distinguish between inquire for a formal investigation and enquire for an informal question. Whereas in Australia, according to Kate Burridge, it's the other way round: 'Enquiry has a more formal ring, rather than inquiry as in the United Kingdom.' In the US inquiry is used in all cases; this is recommended in Britain, too.

insinuate

means more than imply: it includes the idea of something unpleasant or underhand. So this reference to England's rugby captain is wrong:

[Martin Johnson] has insinuated that his time will soon be up.
(*Times*)

install, installation, instalment

are the British spellings.

instep

according to usage, the underneath arched part of the foot (though dictionaries define it as the whole of the foot between ankle and toes).

instil, instilled, instilling

are the British spellings.

insure *see* ensure, insure

interment, internment

to inter is to bury; to intern is to imprison without trial (but see **intern, internee, internist**).

intern, internee, internist

an intern is an American trainee on work experience (eg Monica Lewinsky); an internee is a person interned; an internist is a doctor specialising in internal diseases, a physician rather than a surgeon.

internet

is one word without a cap.

interpretive

not interpretative

into

is sometimes but not always one word: distinguish between 'They came into the house' and 'They came in to dinner.' Some people object to 'They're into jazz' (meaning they like it) so don't use this expression in formal writing.

intoxicated

is literary for drunk.

invalid

as an adjective is pronounced differently according to whether it means sick (stress on 'in') or not valid (stress on 'val').

invaluable

means not able to be valued, ie very valuable, not the opposite of valuable: to be clear, use something else like priceless.

invariably

is a rhetorical adverb used to mean usually as in this example quoted by Bryson:

> Supersede is yet another word that is invariably misspelt.
> (*Chicago Tribune*)

As he says, the literal meaning of invariably is in a fixed and constant way. But it is pedantic to object to this usage. On the other hand, it is not pedantic to object to 'almost invariably' which occurs in Trask's book *Mind the Gaffe*:

> Journalistic prose almost invariably uses *The media is*.

Almost invariably, like almost literally, is nonsense. See **rhetorical adverbs**.

invoke
call upon or appeal for help or inspiration, is confused with evoke, call something up in somebody's mind:

> [The word dag] perhaps invokes a type of eccentric encountered in the wool industry.
>
> (Kate Burridge)

involve
is a loose word, often lazily used when a more precise word is available:

> There was a collision involving two cars.

'Between' would be better here. By contrast,

> No other vehicle was involved

is a stock police phrase it is difficult to object to.

> He is involved with the new company.

'Works for' would be better here.

But if you can't be precise about a relationship, there's a case for involve:

> He is involved [in some unspecified way] with the new company.

Involve is also useful in the sense of include, entangle:

> He tried to involve me in his scheme.

And the adjective involved also means complicated:

> He put forward a very involved argument.

But complicated, being clearer, is better.

ironic

not ironical: see **irony**

ironically *see* **irony**

irony

refers to a contrast between the words used by a speaker or writer and their intended meaning. In some cases the two meanings are clear opposites: the name given to Robin Hood's lieutenant Little John was ironic because he was a giant of a man.

Irony is also used to describe 'a condition in which one seems to be mocked by fate or the facts' (Chambers). From this second sense ironic and ironically are loosely extended to mean strange(ly), paradoxical(ly), even interesting(ly) etc. This usage irritates purists, pedants and a lot of perfectly normal people. *See also*: **sarcasm**.

–ise

not –ize but capsize takes the z.

italic type

is overused both for emphasis and to mark foreign words. In ordinary writing words that need italics because they are obscure should be translated into English.

its/it's *see* **apostrophes**

J

jail, jailer
not gaol, gaoler

jargon
the word is always derogatory, although qualifying it in some way –
sociologists' jargon, medical jargon – reduces the gravity of the
offence. Essentially, jargon is unintelligible (and usually ugly)
vocabulary, especially that used by people like civil servants,
politicians, social workers and academics when speaking or writing
to the rest of us. Every activity – work, sport, art – is inclined to
develop a specialised terminology which practitioners use when
speaking or writing to one another. It becomes jargon when it is used
in a general context. Words like legalese, computerspeak and
psychobabble express the general hostility to jargon.

jealousy *see* **envy, jealousy**

jejune
from the Latin *jejenus* (fasting) is literary for meagre, insipid; it is also
used – pretentiously and wrongly – to mean puerile (possibly because
of confusion with the French word *jeune*, young). A word to be
avoided: use meagre, insipid, puerile instead.

jewellery
not jewelry (except in the US)

jobless *see* **journalese**

John o'Groat's
should theoretically have two apostrophes, since it was originally John of Groat's house. See **apostrophes**.

Johns Hopkins
the university and medical centre in Baltimore, Maryland, has two s's and no apostrophe.

join together
to join two things is to bring them together, so the word together is redundant after join (although it appears in the marriage service).

jokey
not joky

Joneses
is the plural of Jones so you keep up with the Joneses.

journalese
according to Chambers, is the jargon of bad journalism. Words like slam and axe, clampdown and breakthrough, jobless and workshy should be avoided.

judgment
not judgement

judicial, judicious
judicial refers to judges and the system of justice in general; judicious is having sound judgment. So a judge's decisions may be judicious but are always judicial.

just deserts *see* deserts, desserts

K

kaput
from the German *kaputt*, means broken, ruined.

Kashmir *see* **cashmere, Kashmir**

ketchup
not catchup, catsup

kids
the colloquial word for children, is now used by teachers and educationists in formal contexts as a matter of policy. Calling children kids is intended to suggest a matey attitude towards them. This usage irritates many oldfashioned parents whose teachers were more formal.

kind, kinds
kind is singular so it should be 'This kind of person'; kinds is plural so it should be 'These kinds of people'. So 'These are the kind of people' is wrong: it should be 'These are the kinds of people'.

kith and kin
kith originally meant friends; kin is a bit archaic but still a recognisable word for relatives; the phrase kith and kin is obsolete. Use friends and relatives if that is what you mean.

kitsch
is literary for trash(y):

the passions aroused by the kitsch competition.
(*Guardian* report of Miss World)

knelt

not kneeled

knickers *see* **pants**

knit, knitted

use knit as the adjective for united as in 'A closely knit group'; knitted for things made of wool ('a knitted waistcoat').

knock up

once meant to wake (somebody) up and still means to call on voters on polling days and to practise before playing a game of tennis; it also means (as in the US) to make pregnant.

knot

means the speed of one nautical mile per hour, so 'knots per hour' is nonsense: a ship travels at 10 knots.

Knut (King) *see* **Canute (King)**

koala

should not be followed by bear since the koala is a marsupial not a bear.

kudos

meaning praise, is singular.

L

lachrymal
is literary for tearful.

lacuna
from Latin, is literary for some uses of gap. If you want an impressive-sounding word, hiatus, another Latin word, is more familiar, but gap is better.

laissez-faire
not laisser-faire for a non-interventionist policy (and if you use them, laissez-aller, meaning lack of restraint, and laissez-passer for a special permit or pass).

lambast
not lambaste

Land-Rover *see* Range Rover

largesse
not largess for generosity

last, latest, past
last can mean either final or most recent/previous:

His last words were hardly heard. (final)

This speech is better than his last. (previous)

Since 'his last speech' can be ambiguous, prefer 'his latest/most recent speech' if he is still alive and speaking.

'He spoke to me last week' is clear, and so usually is 'He spoke to me in the last few days', but purists prefer 'in the past few days' to avoid suggesting 'the last few days of his life'. It's a logical distinction but not very useful since most people don't make it.

Latin America *see* South, Latin America

Latinisms

should be avoided except in specialised contexts – even the law now struggles to speak English instead of Latin. Phrases like *laudator temporis acti* for somebody who praises the past or *carpe diem* for enjoy the present should be avoided unless your main intention is to impress.

Of the various Latin abbreviations used in English, three are very common and generally understood: etc (and the rest), eg (for example) and ie (that is), though some people confuse the last two. But except in specialised contexts avoid *cf* (compare), *viz* (namely), *et al* (and other people) and the rest.

latter *see* former

lavatory *see* u/non-u

lavish

you lavish praise on somebody rather than lavish them with praise so the following newspaper reference to asylum seekers is wrong:

> Instead of lavishing them with cash and housing them in luxurious council accommodation ...

lay, lie

traditionally, lay and lie are two separate words (though lay is the past tense of lie: 'I lay down').

Lay is a transitive verb so it has an object: you lay the table (present), laid the table (past), have laid the table (past participle).

Lie is intransitive: you lie on the floor (present), lay on the floor (past), have lain on the floor (past participle).

(Lie meaning to tell lies is different again: lie becomes lied in both past and past participle.)

Confusion between lay and lie is common, partly because in the US lay is often used instead of lie:

> Eddy went forward and laid down.
>
> (Hemingway, quoted by Partridge)

> Lay, lady, lay, lay across my big brass bed.
>
> (Bob Dylan)

And the Australian Peter Fitzsimons wrote: 'Nancy's thoughts turned to what might lay before her.'

But the distinction still matters to most users of standard English in Britain.

lead, led
lead pronounced 'led' is the metal; when pronounced 'leed' it is the present tense of the verb to lead, whose past tense is led.

leading question
a leading question is not hostile or unfair to the person it's directed to. It's a question that suggests an appropriate answer. A barrister who says to a witness: 'You saw what happened, didn't you?' expects the answer yes and is leading the witness.

leant
not leaned

leapt
not leaped

learn
is confused with teach:

> How we 'learn' people their language explains much about the attitudes they have toward it.
>
> (Ronald Wardhaugh)

See **mirror words**.

learned, learnt

learned, pronounced as a two-syllable word with a stress on the -ed, means knowledgeable; learnt is the preferred past tense of learn.

learning curve

is management, personnel and training jargon for experience, progress:

> That tour was a great learning curve for me.
> (rugby player Lewis Moody)

least

avoid the double superlative in 'least worst'; prefer least bad.

leisurely *see* **-ly adverbs**

lend

is confused with borrow:

> Engines would attend Southgate Fire Station from far-flung stations to lend pornographic videos from a library in the locker room.
>
> (*Times*)

See **mirror words**.

leporine

is literary for 'of or resembling the hare' and has nothing to do with rabbits, which is a dismissive term for weak tailend batsmen in cricket. If 'hare' means anything in this context, it suggests a fast-scoring batsman, so the following is as nonsensical as it is possible to be:

> Hoggard may be leporine when it comes to batting (batting at no 11 he had scored 17 out of a last-wicket stand of 91; his previous highest test score was 12).
>
> (*Sunday Times*)

lèse-majesté

not lese-majesty

less *see* **fewer, less**

let alone
means 'not to mention, much less' and shouldn't be used to mean 'even more':

> Glenn McGrath learnt his cricket in the bush, hundreds of miles from the city, let alone an academy.
> (David Gower, *Sunday Times*)

> Ankara, let alone that great city of European civilisation, Constantinople – today Istanbul – lie to the west of the Urals.
> (Labour minister Denis MacShane, writing in the *Observer*)

letting go *see* **euphemism**

leukaemia
not leukemia

liaison
is often misspelt: note the two i's. It means relationship (eg military or sexual) not assignation or encounter, so the following is either nonsense or more suggestive than the writer intends:

> Her former lover, with whom she had arranged their liaisons as they sat next to each other during question time, was 'a lovely man'.
> (*Guardian*)

libel, slander
libel is published defamation, which can be either printed or broadcast (or posted on a website), whereas slander is spoken.

licence, license
in British English licence is the noun, license the verb.

lie *see* **lay, lie**

life

the plural of life is lives except for still lifes, paintings of inanimate objects.

lighted, lit

in British English lit is the usual past tense (he lit a cigarette) and lighted the usual adjective (he used a lighted match). But note the exception:

It happened in a well-lit room.

lightening, lightning

lightening is making something lighter; lightning comes with thunder.

like

is there a grammatical problem if the informal like is used instead of the formal such as? Not according to the austere and conservative *Economist Style Guide* which says:

Authorities like Fowler and Gowers is an acceptable alternative to authorities such as Fowler and Gowers.

To avoid confusion between two similar-sounding uses of like, put commas round a comparison but not an example.

Comparison: Politicians, like secondhand-car dealers, struggle with the truth.

Example: Politicians like Prescott struggle with their sentences.

Commas are also essential to clarify the trendy parenthetical use of like as a filler:

He's, like, a clever politician.

This means that, in the speaker's opinion, he really is one, whereas 'He's like a clever politician' would be a comparison.

If like (so to say, as it were) comes at the end of the sentence instead of in the middle – as it does in various country dialects – it still needs a comma:

It's comfortable, like.

Like to mean as or as though is increasingly common:

They didn't talk like other people talked.
(Martin Amis)

It looks like it's still a fox.
(*New Yorker*)

The retsina flowed like the Arno did when it overflowed in 1966.
(*Spectator*)

This usage has traditionally been considered illiterate and unacceptable in writing, eg by Fowler and the *Economist Style Guide*. But Burchfield in his revised edition of Fowler refuses to condemn it and provides various quotes (eg those above) in its defence. If you want to write like most other people – including some very good writers – you'll have no problem with this usage.

But there is one clear misuse of like that can never be justified. This is when it introduces a dangling modifier:

Like a lot of upper-middle-class radicals from Kim Philby to Perry Anderson, there were various non-English strains in his background.
(*London Review of Books*)

This should be either 'as with' instead of 'like' or 'he had' instead of 'there were'.

likeable
not likable

likely

is an adjective meaning probable and in the US (and countries like Israel) an adverb meaning probably:

> If Jesus were alive today the US state department would likely criticise him for being a Jewish settler.
>
> *(Jerusalem Post)*

But in traditional British usage, for some strange reason, likely when used as an adverb has to be qualified in some way. So you can say that the state department would quite likely/very likely/more likely/most likely/more than likely/as likely as not criticise Jesus – but not that it would likely criticise him.

There are signs of the American usage being adopted in Britain:

> Something is happening to our society which is likely unstoppable.
>
> (John Lloyd of the *New Statesman* writing in the London *Evening Standard*)

It's difficult to object to it on logical grounds.

linage, lineage

linage is the number of lines of printed matter; lineage is ancestry.

linchpin

not lynchpin

link together

to link two things is to bring them together so the word together is redundant after link.

liqueur, liquor

a liqueur is a sweetened, flavoured spirit like Cointreau; liquor is a general word for spirits, also used for particular liquids, eg 'oysters in their own liquor'.

lit *see* **lighted, lit**

literally

features in all style and usage guides. Don't use it when you don't mean it, they say. 'He literally exploded with anger' is absurd. But do use it if you need to make clear that a stale metaphor is, for once, an accurate statement. 'He literally died laughing' could be true.

Most published uses of literally fail the test:

> In the Austenian economy, a woman's face is literally her fortune.
>
> (Naomi Wolf, *Sunday Times*)

> Eyewitness accounts of this practice are literally blood-curdling.
>
> (*Times*)

> The more satire there is, the less effect it has. We are all literally deafened.
>
> (Libby Purves, *Times*)

> Kate's tummy has been literally sliced off, leaving her looking positively concave.
>
> (The *Daily Mail* describes the retouching of a photograph of Kate Winslet)

Some people are aware of the problem. As Zadie Smith has one of her characters say: 'Only idiots use the word "literally" in conversation.'

Others seem to think that by putting 'almost' in front of 'literally' they can make it work:

> The people of the rebuilt Oradour lived, almost literally, within this history.
>
> (Adam Nossiter)

> The network was making so much money that it almost literally didn't know what to do with it.
>
> (Mark Lawson)

Rock stars and actors – the people we rely on to flout

convention on principle – get married every day. Some of
them almost literally every day.

(*Guardian*)

Aunt Rose has a body almost literally eaten into by history.

(James Wood)

But how can something be 'almost literally' true? Either it is true or it
isn't. And the same applies to 'more or less':

I grew up in a church that more or less literally invented the
mea culpa.

(*New York Times*)

At first glance Salman Rushdie has a case for 'perhaps' in:

Bronislawa had exhausted three judges and four lawyers. Of
this she had become (perhaps literally) insanely proud.

But the character is either insane or not: 'perhaps literally' is a pointless
parenthesis which reminds us that 'insanely proud' is usually a
metaphor.

Because literally is so generally misused, some people feel that they
have to add an intensifier like 'quite' – to say 'I really mean it':

Conformity was encouraged by uniformity – quite literally, in
the manner of dress.

(*Sunday Times*)

Those Englishmen in the year 1000 who believed quite
literally in the little people, the fairies, trolls and elves.

(Tom Wolfe)

In turn 'quite literally' becomes the standard phrase:

Clinton was quite literally too clever by half.

(*Sunday Times*)

This is where you go quite literally mad with grief.

(magazine editor Lindsay Nicholson)

And so for people who want to say 'I really mean it', a further intensifier is needed. Both examples come from the *Guardian*:

Lee Westwood has backed himself to win the Sun City Golf Challenge after an abysmal year by his standards. Quite literally, in fact. The Worksop player put a sizeable wager on himself.

In Sicily one Vittorio Greco has gone to his grave. Quite literally, in fact: Vittorio was checking progress on a family tomb when he slipped, struck his head and died on the spot.

Quite literally, in fact – or literally, literally, literally. Why not give this word a rest?

livid
originally of a lead colour, means very angry.

loan
in British English loan is traditionally the noun and lend the verb but loan is increasingly used of formal agreements. Footballers are loaned by one club to another and pictures are loaned by private collectors to art galleries:

These works have been loaned from prestigious public and private collections.

(*Guardian*)

But it should be 'loaned by' (or 'borrowed from') – see **lend**.

loath, loathe, loth
loath not loth to mean unwilling, reluctant; loath is confused with loathe, dislike intensely.

Londonderry

is the British (and Ulster Unionist) name for the Irish city of Derry.

loo *see* **u/non-u**

Lord Copper *see* **up to a point, Lord Copper**

Lords

House of Lords but Lord's cricket ground (originally owned by Thomas Lord)

lovable

not loveable

lunch

not luncheon in the 21st century (but for some mysterious reason, luncheon vouchers)

luxuriant, luxurious, luxury

luxuriant means rich in the sense of profuse (luxuriant vegetation) whereas luxurious means rich and lavish (a luxurious house). But the most common adjective from luxury now is – luxury (luxury apartment, coach, cruise etc). No room for confusion here.

-ly adverbs

do not need to be followed by a hyphen so a closely knit group (but a close-knit group).

Words like friendly, leisurely, lonely, lovely, manly, silly make awkward adverbs. The choice is between retaining the same form (he walked leisurely down the street) and adding -ly (he behaved sillily). Both are in the dictionary; neither quite works. Gingerly is said to exist as both adjective and adverb but the adverb is common, the adjective not. Kindly is an -ly word that is idiomatically both adjective and adverb (a kindly word, kindly said). The reason is that the adjective has two forms, kind and kindly.

To avoid the problem, use 'in a friendly/leisurely way'.

M

macerate *see* **marinade, marinate**

mackintosh
(no cap, mac for short) is the standard spelling for a type of raincoat (though the person who gave his name to it was Charles Macintosh).

mad
now means angry in Britain as well as the US.

madeira cake, wine
no cap

magistrates court
needs no apostrophe.

major
as Burchfield points out, has certain idiomatic uses (a major road as opposed to a minor one, major political parties as opposed to minor ones). But it is overused in expressions like 'major road improvement', 'major political scandal' and 'major breakthrough' – what would a minor breakthrough be? If it means anything it's usually just big.

majority
is overused in phrases like 'the majority of cases'. 'It happens in the majority of cases' means 'It usually happens'. Bryson has fun with this word, finding examples of this usage by authorities like Fowler and Partridge and commenting: 'Even when written by the most

discriminating writers, "the vast majority of" seldom says more in four words than "most" says in one.'

Majority is misused in sentences like 'The majority of the book was unreadable' and 'The majority of the meal was inedible.' Majority can only be used of countable things.

In politics (and vote-counting in general) a majority means the greater number of votes. In a British election a candidate who gains more votes than any other wins by a majority of X. This is the difference between the number of votes cast for the winner and the number cast for the runner-up. A winner with more than half the votes has an absolute majority. By contrast, in the US and Canada only an absolute majority is called a majority; a relative majority is called a plurality.

malapropism

from Mrs Malaprop in Sheridan's play *The Rivals* (1775) who was apt to misapply long words in a ludicrous way, as in 'a nice derangement of epitaphs' for 'arrangement of epithets'. A malapropism goes beyond standard confusion (militate/mitigate, prevaricate/procrastinate) and is memorable because it is funny, as in this example from Jilly Cooper quoted by Burchfield:

> When she heard our Gloucester house was haunted, she uttered the immortal line 'You'll have to get the vicar in to circumcise [exorcise] it.'

malapropos

is the English for the French phrase *mal à propos*. Originally an adverb meaning inappropriately (you spoke malapropos), it can also be an adjective, out of place (your words were malapropos).

manhood

is a euphemism for penis, traditionally used by tabloid newspapers but also by novelists:

> Rebecca averted her eyes from the evidence of the Father's manhood.

> (Doris Lessing)

There was certainly nothing wrong with Lars Ericson's manhood. It grew from him like the sturdy limb of a tree.

(Richard Yates)

manifestos
not manifestoes

mankind
to include women prefer humanity (not humankind).

manly *see* **-ly adverbs**

mantelpiece, mantle
a mantelpiece (also mantelshelf and sometimes plain mantel) is a shelf over a fireplace; a mantle is a cloak.

manuscript
a manuscript (something written by hand) is not a typescript, still less something generated on a computer keyboard.

many *see* **few, little**

marijuana
not marihuana

marinade, marinate
meat or fish is marinated (soaked) in a marinade, a mixture of wine/ vinegar, oil, herbs and spices. Fruit is macerated, soaked in alcohol and sugar.

Marseille
not Marseilles

martial
not marshal in martial arts

Mary Celeste

not Marie for the American brigantine whose passengers and crew disappeared during a crossing of the Atlantic in 1872

masterful, masterly

the traditional distinction is clear. Masterful means dominating; masterly means very skilful.

masterful:

> Pop stood short but masterful in the sweaters, and his belly sticking out, not soft but hard.
>
> (Saul Bellow)

masterly:

> The late Alan Clarke's remorseless and masterly TV movie, *The Firm*.
>
> (Martin Amis)

But masterful is often used to mean masterly:

> The Bordeaux wine aristocracy, the people François Mauriac mocked for their masterful palates and empty heads.
>
> (Adam Nossiter)

> Nabokov composed or at any rate completed *The Event* rather later on, in 1938, by which time he had such masterful novels as *The Defence* and *Laughter in the Dark* well behind him.
>
> (Martin Amis again)

In some cases it is difficult to be sure which of the two meanings is intended:

> That Gordon Brown is an excellent chancellor is beyond doubt: towering, masterful, formidable are the adjectives frequently used to describe him.
>
> (*Guardian*)

Excellent suggests masterly (very skilful) but towering and formidable suggest masterful (dominating).

> Hick will continue to look for flat tracks on which to do his masterful bullying.
>
> > *(Observer)*

Bullying suggests masterful (dominating) but if bullying is by definition masterful, the meaning could be masterly (very skilful). The ex-England cricketer Graham Hick was still in 2003 a highly successful batsman so masterly is probable.

As so often with problem words of this kind the real difference between dominating and very skilful is obscured by the current use of masterful. If there is any risk of ambiguity, find another word.

masterfully

Burchfield makes the point that the adverb masterfully is a natural formation 'in regular use since the 14c' whereas masterly as an adverb and the unused masterlily are both awkward (see **-ly adverbs**). Certainly it's easy to find examples of masterfully meaning in a very skilful way. Here are two, both from the *London Review of Books*:

> The sunny central story, masterfully controlled.
> > (James Wood)

> [Ian McEwan's] own prose style – masterfully crafted and unnervingly exact.
> > (Terry Eagleton)

But if masterfully can also mean in a dominating way, it has the same disadvantage as masterful. Again, if there is any risk of ambiguity, find another word.

masterly *see* **masterful, masterly**

matinee

no accent

may, can, might

once upon a time pedagogic parents made their children ask for permission to leave the table. When the child said 'Can I get down?' they were told: 'Of course you can; the question is whether you may.' This distinction between can (physical possibility) and may (permission) is still observed by some. For example, companies keen to impress will train their staff to introduce themselves to customers with 'My name is Sharon; how may I help you?' But most people now say and write 'Can I help you?' without being misunderstood.

Technically, may can convey either permission or possibility: 'He may come' can mean either that he has permission to come or that it's possible he will. This helps to explain why most people say and write 'He can come' (permission)/'He may come' (possibility).

The really important distinction is not between can and may but between may and might. In the present using might makes a possibility weaker: 'I might come' is less likely than 'I may come'. But in the past only might can be used: 'He said he may come' should be 'He said he might come'.

Even more important is the may have/might have distinction. 'He may have come' can only mean that we don't know whether he did or not. 'He might have come' means that he didn't come, but if things had been different, perhaps he would have. This critical distinction is constantly ignored:

> Jesus may or may not have joined a No Shopping Day protest, but Karl Marx would not have.
>
> *(Times)*

No, we know that Jesus didn't. It should be 'Jesus might or might not have ...'

After heavy rain fell near Twickenham but not on it, Norman Harris wrote in the *Observer*:

> Whether that meant that God was smiling on England at Twickenham was hard to say, for the home side may well have benefited from soggy going.

It's a convoluted point sabotaged by the failure to use 'might have'. The going was not soggy – it did not rain at Twickenham – so England didn't benefit from it. It should be 'the home side might well have benefited'.

me *see* **I/me**

media
is the plural of medium so it should be 'The media are held responsible for the ills of modern Britain'. But more and more the media takes on a singular form because it is seen as a single entity like the hydra, a monster with many heads. So it's difficult to object to 'The media is responsible for the ills ...' The plural form is better, though, and will offend nobody.

Where media is used to mean individual journalists as in this *Times* headline: 'Media outnumber mourners as Hindley is cremated', the plural is essential. In this report (also from the *Times*) the plural used at the beginning degenerates to the singular:

> You can imagine the stink if the media are banned in two and a half months ... Then came the news that the media was not welcome.

It should be 'the media were not welcome'.

medieval
not mediaeval

mediums
is the plural of medium meaning a person who claims to communicate with spirits.

meet
not meet with, meet up with, which are American

melee
no accents

mementoes
not mementos

memorandums, memos
are the plurals of memorandum, memo; see **plurals**.

menage

(but ménage à trois) – see **accents**

meretricious

is literary for trashy (originally it meant worthy of a prostitute).

mésalliance

means marriage with a social inferior, whereas misalliance means any unsuitable union, particularly marriage.

metal, mettle

these are two different spellings of what was once the same word. Use metal for the substance (gold, lead), mettle for temperament, spirit, courage.

metaphor, simile

are two similar figures of speech. Whereas metaphor is calling something by the name of what it resembles, simile is likening it to something. A simile is introduced by like or as; a metaphor is not. ('My love is like a rose' is a simile; 'My love is a rose' is a metaphor.)

Because they are similar, they are often confused:

> She burst like a comet into the skies of academic English scholarship – with her brilliant red-gold hair, comet is an apt metaphor.
>
> *(Guardian)*

Like a comet is a simile.

Mixing metaphors is inept and usually makes what you say or write sound ridiculous:

> He has been made a sacrificial lamb for taking the lid off a can of worms.
>
> *(Times*, quoted by Burchfield)

> 'You must forgive the new broom. I have to learn the ropes,' he added getting confused among the metaphors.
>
> (Graham Greene, quoted by Longman)

In many common phrases which are metaphorical in origin the metaphor is effectively dead (she sat at the foot of the table; he flew into a rage). But the metaphor can be revived by the addition of a badly chosen word:

> There are several concrete steps we can take.
> (Anita Roddick)

First build your concrete steps.

meter, metre
meter for a measuring instrument (gas meter) but metre (and centimetre etc) for a unit of length.

meticulous
once meant timid, then over-careful about minute details. Now it means 'careful, punctilious, scrupulous, precise' (Burchfield). The over-careful usage exists mainly in dictionaries and usage guides.

microbe *see* bacterium, bug, microbe, virus

midday
not mid-day

middle ages
no caps

middle class
is misused to mean posh, which irritates careful readers:

> Ed Stourton may be 'too posh' and perhaps 'middle-aged' but he is certainly not 'middle-class' ... he is distinctly aristocratic.
> (*Guardian* letter)

Middlesbrough
is often misspelt; it is not like Peterborough or Edinburgh.

might *see* **may, can, might**

mileage
not milage

militate *see* **mitigate, militate**

millennium
not millenium, milennium

minimal
'minimal accuracy is required' means at least some accuracy not the least possible.

minority ethnic
the two words ethnic minority are sometimes transposed in phrases like 'the position of minority ethnic women'. A pointless variation – avoid.

minuscule
not miniscule

mirror words
describe the same action or relationship from two opposite points of view: if I lend you something, you borrow it. But some people substitute borrow for lend:

> Can I lend your book, please?

Other common pairs often confused are: teach/learn, infer/imply, ancestor/descendant.

misalliance *see* **mésalliance**

mischievous
not mischievious

mislead
there is no such word as misle, which is wrongly formed from misled.

Miss *see* **Ms**

misspell
not mispell

mistakable
not mistakeable

mitigate, militate
to mitigate is to soften, reduce the effect of (mitigating circumstances);
to militate against something is to have a harmful effect on it. Militate
is followed by against; mitigate is not. Mitigate is often used mistakenly
instead of militate:

> 'Busy' mitigates against patience, tolerance, consideration.
> (*Guardian*)

> Edward sat between Zoë and Angela, which she thought
> would mitigate against the elderly elements of the party.
> (Elizabeth Jane Howard)

In the second case mitigate is right but against should be deleted.

mixed metaphor *see* **metaphor, simile**

Moby-Dick
Melville's whale novel, has a hyphen.

Mohammed *see* **Muhammad**

moot
is literary for debatable:

> Practically, the call to lift the pension age to 70 is pretty moot.
> (*Times* letter)

mortality *see* **fatality, mortality**

mosquitoes
not mosquitos

mottoes
not mottos

movable
not moveable though Hemingway described Paris as 'a moveable feast'

mph
no full stops

Mr, Mrs *see* **Ms**

Ms
women's forms of address remain a problem despite the introduction of Ms. This was intended to replace Miss and Mrs, which show a woman's marital status, and become the equivalent of Mr. But many British women don't call themselves Ms and would prefer not to be addressed as such. So when writing to or about a stranger it's probably safer to use no title at all, particularly since titles generally are used less and less.

much less
is similar to let alone: to work it needs to follow a negative:

> I didn't see him, much less have a drink with him.

It is often confused with even/much more:

> Black students ostracised other blacks who dated (much less married) whites.
>
> *(Atlantic Monthly)*

See **let alone**.

Muhammad
not Mahomet, Mohammed

Muslim
not Moslem, Muhammadan

mutual

is more of a problem for the writers of usage guides than it is for writers in general. The traditional view is that mutual should only be used to mean reciprocal: 'Their dislike was mutual' says of two people that each disliked the other. According to this view, the expression 'our mutual friend' to mean a friend we have in common is incorrect. This would put all sorts of otherwise literate people (including Shakespeare and Charles Dickens, who used the phrase as a title) in the naughty corner.

Which is ridiculous. Clearly, in the real world, mutual is used to mean either reciprocal or common. Usually the context will show which is intended but if there is a risk of ambiguity, use reciprocal or common instead.

A reason for not using common is that it can mean inferior: 'our common friend' could appear derogatory (while 'the friend we have in common' is longwinded). A reason for not using reciprocal is that it can mean something more than mutual, as Longman points out. 'I dislike her and she reciprocates/has a reciprocal attitude to me' suggests that I started it whereas 'We have a mutual dislike' does not.

myself

has two accepted uses: as an emphatic form of **I/me** (I couldn't understand it myself) and as a reflexive (I try not to contradict myself). It is also misused as a substitute for I/me, often because the speaker/writer seems to feel that I/me would be too direct:

The director and myself will be there.

Please inform the director and myself.

Use I in the first case, me in the second.

N

naive
not naif, naïf, naïve

naivety
not naïvety, naïveté, naiveté, naivete

napkin, serviette
(table) napkin as opposed to serviette is one of the few surviving u/ non u distinctions (see **u/non-u**). Use napkin.

Native Americans
is now the approved word for the indigenous population of the US but children still play cowboys and Indians.

naturalist, naturist
a naturalist studies natural history; naturist is another name for nudist.

naught, nought
naught is literary for nothing (our hopes came to naught); nought is zero (a batsman is out for nought).

nauseated, nauseating, nauseous
come from nausea, which originally meant sea-sickness. Nauseating is sick-making and (metaphorically) disgusting:

The meal was nauseating. (It made me feel sick.)

His behaviour was nauseating. (It disgusted me.)

To be nauseated is to be sick or disgusted:

I was nauseated by the prawns. (I felt sick.)

I was nauseated by his behaviour. (It disgusted me.)

Nauseous has traditionally been an alternative to nauseating in the literal sense:

The meal was nauseous. (It made me feel sick.)

It is now also used as an alternative to nauseated:

The meal made me (feel) nauseous.

Because they are clearer, prefer nauseating/nauseated.

naval, navel
naval refers to the navy, navel to the belly button; hence the navel orange, which has a navel-like depression enclosing a small internal, embryonic fruit.

nearby
is one word.

necessary
not neccessary

née
which is French for born, is the conventional way of introducing a married woman's maiden name: (Mrs) Mary Smith, née Jones. Note that née, with the extra e, is the feminine form; né is not commonly used.

negative, double *see* double negative

négligé
for a woman's light dressing-gown, not négligée, negligee

Negro, Negress *see* **black**, **feminine forms**

neither *see* **either, neither**

nemesis
from the Greek goddess, is literary for retribution or the agent of retribution; it should not be used for a mere rival or enemy; and it does not mean opposite as it appears to here:

> Haider's nationalism is the nemesis of her internationalism.
> (*Bulletin*)

neologism
is literary and derogatory for a new word or phrase.

neophyte
is literary for beginner.

nerve-racking *see* **rack, wrack**

net
not nett for the opposite of gross

never
can trip the most distinguished writers. William Safire of the *New York Times* wrote the following (and later apologised for his mistake):

> The *New York Times*, which willingly corrects itself when in error, does not settle libel suits for money. *Never.*

It should be ever.

nevertheless
is one word.

new

this word is often redundant. In general, if something is being reported (whether in the media or not), it's likely to be new – otherwise why report it? Bryson quotes a choice double example from the *New York Times*:

New Boom for Florida Creates New Concerns

news

is singular: the news is good.

new year

but New Year's Day, Eve

next

used before the days of the week, usually means the one that follows, so 'next Saturday' means the first Saturday after today. But in Scotland and parts of northern England 'next Saturday' can mean the Saturday of next week as opposed to this (coming) Saturday.

nice

there is nothing wrong with this word, whether used to mean pleasant (a nice man, a nice day) or its opposite (a nice mess) or exact (a nice distinction) but lazy writers overuse it.

niceish

not nicish – but it's an ugly word.

niece

not neice

niggardly *see* **nigger**

nigger

has become the most taboo word in English (though some black people in the US continue to use it about themselves). For example, nigger brown is not now acceptable to mean a dark-brown colour.

Here's a sentence from a short story by Saul Bellow first published in 1957 and anthologised in 2001:

> In those little bungalows Poles, Swedes, micks, spics, Greeks and niggers lived out their foolish dramas of drunkenness, gambling, rape, bastardy, syphilis and roaring death.

It's difficult to imagine that sentence being written by a white writer today. The word nigger is now so powerful that even its echo can condemn the user: the black mayor of Washington DC is said to have fired a white aide in 1999 for using the word niggardly in a discussion of the city budget. Niggardly, which means stingy, has no connection with nigger.

nigh
is literary for near.

nightdress
is one word.

night–time
not nighttime

nitty–gritty
has been accused of being a racist term (because of an alleged association with slave ships) but all the evidence is the other way. Nitty-gritty, meaning the basics, emerged in the 1960s and has been used in this sense by black people as well as white. Gladys Knight and the Pips had a hit with 'Let's Get Down to the Real Nitty-Gritty' and in 1969 a woman reader wrote to the black American magazine *Ebony*:

> Let's just lay all phony excuses aside and get down to the true nitty-gritty and tell it like it really is. Black males hate black women just because they are black.

noes
not nos

noisome

has nothing to do with noise; it means disgusting.

nom de guerre, plume

are used for somebody who writes under an assumed name. Nom de guerre (literally fighting name) is authentic French but may not be understood by everybody; nom de plume (pen name) is not French but franglais and may make the user appear both pretentious and ignorant. There are two English equivalents, pseudonym and pen name. Since pseudonym can imply false or fictitious, the plain pen name is recommended.

nonce

is archaic for the occasion (for the nonce means for the time being); a nonce word is one coined for the occasion. In prison slang a nonce is a sex offender.

none

the idea that none must be followed by a singular verb is a superstition which seems to be based on the mistaken idea that none means 'not one'. As Longman says: 'None may be followed by a singular or a plural verb as the sense requires.' When none is part of a plural subject the plural verb is usually the natural choice:

> None of the guns were loaded.
> (Donna Tartt)

Of course she could have been more emphatic and written 'Not one of the guns', in which case the verb would have been the singular 'was loaded'.

For some reason the *Guardian* is particularly superstitious in its attitude to none. Its political editor, Michael White, once wrote:

> None of the outraged words published on this row has come anywhere near proving the main charge.

How exactly would a single word prove a charge? The plural would work better here – and in the following from the *London Review of Books*:

Only 6000 US combat soldiers remained in Vietnam and none was involved in the ensuing bloodbath.

(Murray Sayle)

nonetheless
is one word.

non-u *see* **u/non-u**

no one
not no-one, noone

normalcy, normality
normality is the ordinary word; normalcy, which is widely used in the US, is used by some British people but sounds American.

nosy
not nosey

noticeable
not noticable

not un-
this construction (as in not uncommon, not unfriendly) was one of George Orwell's favourite examples of waffle. He wrote:

> One can cure oneself of the not un- formation by memorising this sentence: A not unblack dog was chasing a not unsmall rabbit across a not ungreen field.

Use not un- rarely and always carefully.

nought *see* **naught, nought**

nouveaux riches
is the plural of nouveau riche and should have been used here:

Drug dealers are the nouveau riche in modern Liverpool.

(*Guardian*)

nubile

now means sexy rather than marriable, its original meaning.

nugatory

is literary for trifling, worthless:

They say the benefits of wind power are nugatory.

(John Humphrys, *Sunday Times*)

nul points

as written this is franglais not French. The French for 'no points' is *zero points*. It has been suggested that 'nul points' is in fact misspelt Norwegian – from *null poeng* – and that the phrase came into English after Norway was the first country to be given no points in the Eurovision song contest.

number agreement

the principle of number agreement is obvious and easy to state: a singular subject takes a singular verb; a plural subject takes a plural verb. But there are complications: some subjects are plural in form and essentially singular while others are singular in form and essentially plural.

An example is the word number itself. 'A number is stamped on each computer' is a straightforward singular, as is 'The number of computers needed has gone up.' But 'a number of computers' – meaning many – takes the plural 'are needed'. In the same way expressions like a crowd of people and a gaggle of geese are usually followed by plural verbs:

A jumble of stuffed animals were packed in the bed around her.

(Donna Tartt)

Per cent takes a singular verb when it refers to quantity (20 per cent of his time is spent gardening) but a plural when it refers to number (20 per cent of those polled were in favour). One in five – which means the same thing – also takes the plural:

> Barely one in 50 British families say grace regularly before meals.
>
> (Economist)

But the singular would be used after 'one family in 50':

> Barely one British family in 50 *says* ...

Collective nouns can take either a singular or a plural verb, depending on the sense:

> The team is small (it hasn't got many members).

> The team are small (they aren't very big).

> The board is determined/divided (seen as a single entity).

> The board are agreed/are discussing (seen as separate people).

The two forms should not be used close together. Avoid:

> The board is divided but they are discussing what to do next.

Some plural-sounding words ending in s are singular: news, politics, athletics, measles, billiards, statistics (statistics is my pet subject). In one or two cases they can also be used as plurals (the researcher's statistics were misleading).

Plural phrases which measure or quantify take the singular: 'Five hours is a long time to wait/five miles is a short drive/five pounds is enough.'

Some compound subjects which are thought of as single entities take the singular:

> Rock'n'roll dates back to the 1950s.

His gin and tonic was on the bar.

Law and order is a live issue.

A dozen further points are covered by the Longman guide in a very thorough treatment of number agreement. *See also*: **none**.

numbers

raise various points of house style, eg when to use words and when to use figures. The most common starting point for figures is 10, with numbers up to nine being written out in words; when numbers like nine and 10 appear in the same sentence, nine becomes 9 (9 or 10, 9–10). Some publishers (eg the *Times* and the *Economist*) start their figures at 11, but Trask is wrong to say: 'It is bad style to write *She had 10 children*.' The *Guardian*, Reuters and (in technical writing) the Oxford University Press, among others, start their figures at 10 and this style is recommended.

Commas are used in ordinary writing to mark off thousands: 5,300,200. But in technical writing the commas are replaced by spaces: 5 300 200.

Figures are not used at the beginning of sentences. '25 people were there' becomes 'Twenty-five people ...'

Note the difference between a precise figure (there were 103 people in the room) and an approximation (a hundred people were there). Don't mix them up: 'a 100 people' amounts to saying 'a one hundred people'.

O

obliged

not obligated: the extra syllable adds nothing:

> The truth is I am obligated to be at university for four hours a
> week.
>
> (*Guardian* letter)

oblivious

once meant forgetful and was usually followed by of. Now it means
unaware (whether the person has forgotten whatever it is or never
knew it) and is followed by either of or to:

> He was oblivious of/to his surroundings.

As Burchfield comments, 'The new sense now forms part of the
orthodox vocabulary of any educated person.'

But if you mean forgetful rather than just unaware, don't use
oblivious – use forgetful.

obloquy

is literary for disgrace.

obscene

is overused as a rhetorical adjective meaning 'it offends me'.

'He thinks it's slightly obscene' was a quote about the Prince of
Wales' reaction to caviar costing £10,000 reported in the *Observer*,
while in the *Guardian* Timothy Garton Ash referred to 'material
which, once you know it is fraudulent, is truly obscene'.

obscenity *see* **four-letter words**

observance, observation
observance is observing in the sense of following, carrying out (eg a rule); observation is observing in the sense of seeing, noticing, speaking.

obtuse
which means dense in the sense of stupid, is confused with obscure, opaque:

> She is obtuse about whether or not she's had anything done.
> *(Marie Claire)*

occlude
is literary for shut, cover:

> Every now and then she had to remove her glasses to wipe the mist from them: Tennyson and the hot water combined to occlude.
> (Elizabeth Jane Howard)

oculist, ophthalmologist, optometrist, optician
ophthalmologist (modern) and oculist (oldfashioned) both mean a doctor who specialises in treating eye diseases. Opticians, who supply spectacles and other optical goods, may be ophthalmic (qualified to test eyes and prescribe) or dispensing (not qualified). Optometrist is an American term for ophthalmic optician.

-odd
the hyphen is essential if 20-odd means about 20; '20 odd people' could mean 20 peculiar ones.

of
this little word often turns up where it is not wanted, either as a replacement for an idiomatic preposition (bored of, fed up of instead of with) or as pure padding (all of those present, he got off of the bus, he thinks outside of the box).

off their own bat
(from cricket) is the idiom for doing something unaided, not 'off their own back'.

offence
not offense, which is American

official, officious
official means relating to an office (official title) or authorised (official version); officious means interfering, fussy (officious caretaker).

offspring
is literary for child(ren):

> Parents must suspect that their offspring, who has a home and a job, is having sex regularly.
>
> (*Observer*)

OK
not Ok, ok, okay

older
is the comparative of old (she is older than he is) but it is also used as a euphemism to mean less old than old: 'the older person'. Like most euphemisms this is to be avoided.

O level
with cap but no hyphen for what was the GCE ordinary level examination

omelette
which is French, not omelet, which is American

on, in *see* **in, on**

one
used in the impersonal sense (One cannot complain), is now much less common than 'You can't complain'. If you do decide to use one, you

must persevere with it rather than change to something else. The British mistake is to change from one to you:

> Keeping one's counsel ... takes it out of you.

> If anything unpleasant is written about one then it will be sent to you by some well-wisher.
>
> (both by Doris Lessing)

> The crimes one must now commit, in order to create such a foul stench of horror around yourself ... are truly awful.
>
> (*Observer*)

The American mistake is to change from one to something like he:

> One waits until he is invited to the Algonquin hotel by some senior member of the staff [of the *New Yorker*].
>
> (Tom Wolfe)

It's far simpler to start and continue with you.

one-in-five etc *see* **number agreement**

ongoing
is jargon; prefer continuing.

online
is one word.

only
is a problem word not because of its meaning – which is clear – but because of its disputed position in a sentence. As Burchfield says, 'The placing of only takes one to a front-line battle which has been taking place for more than 200 years.' According to the purists, only should be placed close to the word it qualifies; according to the pragmatists, it should be placed where it naturally falls, between subject and verb, early in a long sentence etc.

To the purists 'You can only die once' should be 'You can die only once'; 'We're only here for the beer' should be 'We're here only for the beer'; and 'The bus only runs on Sundays' should be 'The bus runs only on Sundays.'

In ordinary writing, as in ordinary speech, the pragmatists have the better of the argument since in most cases the sentence reads better with only in its natural place and there is little risk of confusion. But in public notices, as the Longman guide says, there's a strong case for ensuring that the message is clear. 'Cooked shellfish only in this fridge' could mean several different things. 'Only cooked shellfish in this fridge' would tell people to put their raw oysters somewhere else.

onto/on to
is a pair rather like into/in to. Onto should be one word only when it means to a position on (the cat jumped onto the table). In the following example the first 'onto' is right, the second wrong:

> Nancy got onto the Paris Express to take her back to her apartment and then onto England.
>
> (Peter Fitzsimons)

ooh-la-la *see* French

ophthalmologist *see* oculist, ophthalmologist, optometrist, optician

opine
is literary for say.

opposite gender
is jargon; prefer opposite sex.

opposite meanings
various words in English have opposite meanings either because two words of different origin have the same spelling or because the same word can be used in dramatically different ways. For example:

> chuffed: very pleased and disgruntled

> (to) cleave: divide (cleft stick) and stick firmly

(to) dust: clean (remove dust) and sprinkle (eg sugar)

fast: not moving (as in stuck fast) and rapid

(to) head: remove the head/top and supply a head/top

(to) let: allow and prevent

(to) overlook: look over and fail to see

quite: fairly (quite good) and very (quite excellent)

seeded: sown with seed and (of fruit) with the seeds removed

Some words have very different meanings in American and British English. For example:

bomb: to go like a bomb in British is to succeed; to bomb in American is to fail

homely: friendly, kindly in British; ugly in American

(to) table: put something on the agenda in British; take it off the agenda in American.

optician *see* oculist, ophthalmologist, optometrist, optician

optometrist *see* oculist, ophthalmologist, optometrist, optician

oral, verbal
traditionally, oral means spoken (oral examination) and verbal means related to words (verbal reasoning). But 'verbal agreement' is the idiomatic term for one that is spoken not written. There is no ambiguity here since an agreement necessarily involves words.

Another idiom is 'non-verbal communication', the use of gesture and body language instead of words; effectively this means unspoken since it is only used of people in face-to-face contact (who can observe one another's physical behaviour).

ordinance, ordnance
an ordinance is a regulation or decree; ordnance is artillery and the supplies necessary for it.

ordinary
means both normal and by virtue of office so a judge or the Pope has 'ordinary powers', meaning those that come from their office.

orgasmic
is overused for very exciting.

orient, orientate
orient is recommended because it is shorter. So too is disorient rather than disorientate.

Orwellian
a lazy, over-used word that means very little. As the *New Statesman* pointed out, 'People claim to find in [George Orwell's] works support for every position from deep-dyed romanticism to utopian socialism.'

otiose
is literary for superfluous:

> This demand was, as Lord Jenkins would say, otiose.
> (*Guardian*)

> It is otiose to point out that Blair has betrayed the cause of British Europeanism.
> (David Clark, former political adviser)

our mutual friend *see* mutual

overly
is an irritating and pointless variant of over.

Oxford comma *see* **serial comma**

oxymoron(ic)
is literary for a contradiction in terms:

> the oxymoronic 'bootcamp yoga'
> *(Economist)*

P

pace

is literary for despite/with deference to and is traditionally used when (politely and formally) disagreeing with somebody. It looks very silly here:

> In my experience (pace the odd frisky child), you practically have to get out of a car and haul pedestrians across a zebra crossing.
>
> (*Guardian*)

paean, paeon, peon, peony

a paean, originally a song of praise, triumph or thanksgiving, is now literary for any form of praise; a paeon is a metrical foot in classical poetry; a peon is a peasant, day labourer, person of low status, in Latin America or India; a peony is a flower.

paediatrics, paedophilia

not pediatrics, pedophilia, but see **pedagogy, pedantry**

pajamas *see* **pyjamas**

palate, palette, pallet

the palate is the roof of the mouth and so the sense of taste (she has an excellent palate); a palette is the board on which a painter mixes colour and so the range of colours; a pallet is a platform for moving and storing goods and also a mattress.

palpable
is literary for obvious (a palpable lie; in *Hamlet* 'A hit, a very palpable hit').

panacea
a panacea is a cure for all diseases, a solution to all problems, so universal before panacea is redundant.

Panglossian
with cap (from Dr Pangloss in Voltaire's *Candide*) is literary for over-optimistic.

pants
in British English is traditionally short for underpants but it is also the common American word for trousers. There's always the risk of confusion:

> 'In front of everyone,' Nancy recounts, 'Violette and I jumped onto him. I held him down and she took his pants off. In just a few minutes the instructor's pants were flying from the compound flagpole.'
>
> (Australian Nancy Wake tells fellow-Australian Peter Fitzsimons about high jinks during an SOE course in wartime Britain with Violette Szabo)

In British English don't use pants for trousers.

Pants is also slang for something that's no good – avoid in formal writing.

paparazzo
is the singular of paparazzi, photographers who snatch pictures of celebrities.

papier mâché
(moulded paper pulp) is two words and needs both accents.

paradigm
is literary for model, template, blueprint, but it is also used loosely to mean almost anything. Here it seems to mean environment:

The world is operating in a new strategic paradigm. The simultaneous presence of terrorist organisations, weapons of mass destruction and rogue states makes this a new strategic environment.

(*Australian*)

parameter

is a technical term in mathematics (referring to a variable factor constant in a particular case). It is often used as a trendy alternative to limit or boundary, possibly through confusion with perimeter: 'Parameters for "legal" drugs use' was a *Times* headline on a letter which referred to 'appropriate sanctions for those who break the limits'.

We operate within the broad moral parameters of our time … we make an unspoken assumption, as employers of onscreen talent, that these lives are within acceptable parameters.

(ITV boss David Liddiment writing in the *Guardian*)

Use limit or boundary.

partake

(with of) is literary for share in (he partook of our picnic) and a euphemism for drink alcohol:

Nothing was partaken by me.
(Australian politician Steve Bracks)

partly, partially

prefer the more ordinary partly for 'in part' (the house was partly painted). But partially is used to mean 'not fully' as in 'he is partially blind'.

passé

which is literary for out-of-date, needs the acute accent.

passenger action
is the current euphemism on the London Underground for what used to be called 'a person under a train', ie suicide.

passersby
is the plural of passerby.

pate, pâté
the pate is the crown of the head, especially a bald person's; pâté, French for paste, needs both accents.

pathos *see* **bathos**

Pearl Harbour
not Harbor

pedagogy, pedantry
pedagogy is the art or science of teaching; pedantry is excessive concern for trifling details, eg of language. But in British English the distinction between pedagogue and pedant has become blurred, though the two words are not synonymous: pedagogue is always derogatory, though it can suggest strictness and dogmatism as well as pedantry. In American English pedagogue is still used in a neutral way to mean teacher. To be clear, avoid the word pedagogue.

pedal, peddle
to pedal is to ride a bicycle; to peddle is to sell goods from place to place. A travelling vendor is a pedlar in British English but the American peddler is now standard for someone who sells drugs illegally.

pederasty
not paederasty for sexual abuse of a boy by a man

pedlar, peddler *see* **pedal, peddle**

pendant, pendent
a pendant is something hanging, eg an ornament; pendent is the adjective meaning hanging.

penknife

is one word.

penultimate

is literary for second-last (the penultimate paragraph). But we say the last or final, not the ultimate, paragraph. So instead of 'the penultimate', why not say 'the second-last' or 'the last but one'?

people

is the standard plural of person (see **person**) though it is also used as a singular word meaning nation. When you use the possessive, remember to put the apostrophe in the right place, eg 'the people's princess' (unless the princess has been adopted by many peoples, ie nations, in which case 'the peoples' princess' would be right).

per

is overused. Try not to mix Latin and English: he earns £30,000 a year, not per year; she was driving at 80 miles an hour, not per hour. But the abbreviations mpg (miles per gallon) and mph (miles per hour) are accepted usage.

per cent

not percent, per cent. or % (except in tables); see **number agreement**.

perennial/ly

are literary for permanent, always:

> Australia (perennially a racist country, as John Pilger's historical researches have incontrovertibly proved).
>
> (Clive James)

perimeter *see* **parameter**

perpendicular

which means upright, is confused with parallel:

Adjust the seat height so that your thighs are perpendicular to the floor and your feet sit flat on the floor.

(Hewlett-Packard online newsletter giving
advice on choosing an office chair)

person

has two plurals: the standard one, people (three people were killed in the crash) and a formal one, persons (three persons in one god, murder by persons unknown).

-person

is used to replace -man in politically correct speech and writing (chairperson, salesperson, spokesperson). But this is ugly and clumsy: where possible use -woman for women and -man for men:

A spokesman/spokeswoman for the prime minister.

See also: **chair.**

personal

is usually redundant, as in 'a personal friend' (what other kind is there?) and train announcements saying 'Please remember to take your personal belongings with you.'

perspicacious, perspicuous

perspicacious is literary for astute, perspicuous for clear. Be astute and clear: avoid them.

pertain

is literary for belong, apply:

There are only two true engines of radical constitutional change – revolution and national disaster – and neither pertains here.

(London Review of Books)

peruse

is literary for read carefully – and read without qualification. Avoid.

171

petrel, petrol
a petrel is a seabird (storm petrel); petrol, derived from petroleum, is fuel for cars.

phase
to do something by phases, is confused with faze, to disturb, worry:

> Nothing phased you.
> (Doris Lessing)

phenomenon
is the singular of phenomena.

phone
does not need an apostrophe.

phoney
not phony

photocopy
not Photostat or Xerox, which are trade names

pièce de résistance
for the most important item, especially the main dish of a meal, is franglais not French. The French for main dish is *plat de résistance*, while a *pièce montée* is a spectacular pâtisserie.

pikestaff, plain as a
this phrase, which is used to mean obvious, unmistakable, is anything but. It was originally 'plain as a *pack*staff', the staff on which a pedlar carried his pack, worn plain and smooth (Brewer).

pitiable, pitiful
dictionaries don't distinguish between these two but pitiful more often implies contempt:

She earns our sympathy not because she is pitiful but because she is pitiable – and there is a big difference.

(Jeanette Winterson on Dr Zhivago's wife Tonya)

plaster of Paris
one cap

plateaux
is the plural of plateau.

pleonasm *see* **tautology**

plurality *see* **majority**

plurals
there is no hard and fast rule about the plurals of foreign and classical words. Addendum becomes addenda but memorandum becomes memorandums. Bureau, chateau and plateau take the French x, but beau (for boyfriend) is better with the English s, possibly because the word isn't used to mean boyfriend in French.

plus
don't use plus as a trendy alternative to also (he won the race, plus he broke the world record); use and instead.

poetess *see* **feminine forms**

political correctness
it's a principle of good writing that you should write for your readers and not offend them by your choice of words (unless that is your intention). So you should be on the lookout for recommended changes in usage to avoid sexism, racism etc. But be careful. In some cases (eg changing fireman to firefighter) there can hardly be a problem; in others (eg changing prostitute to sex worker) there may be (most people disapprove of prostitution). As Deborah Cameron has pointed out, 'The main effect of the "PC" controversy has been to make every available usage having to do with race or gender politically loaded and thus offensive to somebody.'

polymath

means all-round scholar so all-round before polymath is redundant.

poof, pouf, pouff, pouffe

poof is a derogatory word for a male homosexual; other similar ones are poove and poofter. Use pouf, rather than pouff or pouffe, for a large firm cushion with a solid base, a type of hairstyle or the padded part of a dress (pouffe may look like French but it isn't).

populace, populous

the populace is literary for ordinary people; populous (of a place) means heavily populated.

pore *see* **pour, pore**

portentous, pretentious

portentous can be either ominous (a portentous event) or pompous (his portentous attitude); pretentious means pretending to be important. Since a pretentious person can also be pompous/portentous, there's a risk of confusion with these words. Prefer ominous or pompous to portentous.

poser, poseur

a poser is somebody who poses in the literal sense (an artist's model) and also a puzzle; a poseur is somebody who strikes false attitudes.

postmortem

is one word.

postwar

is one word.

pour, pore

pour (stream) is confused with pore (examine closely):

> Uniformed police poured over the concrete of the car park for traces of blood.
>
> (*Guardian*)

practice, practise
practice is the noun, practise the verb.

practising (homosexuals)
this expression offends gay people. But in the Catholic and Anglican churches it is felt necessary to distinguish between homosexual priests who are sexually active and those who are not. Prefer the term sexually active.

prebook
(to prebook theatre tickets) is a nonsensical extension of book.

precipitate, precipitous
precipitate is literary for sudden, hasty, rash; precipitous is steep (like a precipice). Prefer sudden, hasty or rash to precipitate: they express different shades of meaning and are more widely understood.

precis
does not need an accent.

prefer
in a comparison should be followed by to (I prefer A to B) not than.

premier, premiere
premier is used as a noun to mean prime minister and as an adjective to mean foremost. A premiere (no accent needed) is the first public performance of a film.

premise
not premiss for the singular word meaning something assumed in logic, the basis of an argument. The word premises when used about property is always in the plural (he has bought new premises) even if it refers to a something like a shop.

prepositions
a preposition (from the Latin for placed before) connects a noun, pronoun or other equivalent to another part of the sentence or the sentence as a whole. A preposition usually comes first (he gave it *to* me)

but ending a sentence with a preposition is not bad grammar: this is not something to worry *about*.

prescribe, proscribe
to prescribe is to lay down or specify (a doctor prescribes medicine); to proscribe is to forbid or condemn (a doctor may proscribe smoking).

present
is medical jargon for show (a doctor) symptoms, as in this column by a doctor:

> Somehow the clientele know it wouldn't really work so well presenting to casualty suicidal on the bus at three in the afternoon on a sunny day.
>
> (Michael Foxton)

presently
can mean either soon or now (in Scotland and the US). Use soon or now.

press, pressure, pressurise
the simplest verb meaning to apply pressure is press (he pressed me to agree with him). Or you can write: 'He put pressure on me.' If you feel you have to use either pressure as a verb or pressurise, use the shorter form.

prestigious
now means having or bringing prestige (he lives in a prestigious area); former meanings like juggling and deceitful exist only in reference books.

presumptive, presumptuous
presumptive means giving grounds for presuming (a presumptive heir); presumptuous means presuming too much, so insolent.

preternatural/ly
is literary for abnormal/ly.

prevalence *see* **incidence, prevalence**

prevaricate, procrastinate
prevaricate (evade the truth) is confused with procrastinate (delay):

> It took him some time to choose the neatly sharp suit and his
> chic black Prada shoes. Both the suit and his prevarication, he
> says, are atypical.
>> (*Independent on Sunday Portrait*)

> Late in 1965, after a period of uncertainty and some
> prevarication a majority of the fellows persuaded the college
> to announce that it would open its doors to graduate students.
>> (Dr Bryan Wilson)

> I have promised to bring you to the point of action. But I have
> prevaricated. I have delayed.
>> (John le Carré)

preventive
not preventative, preventitive

previous, prior to
are literary for before.

prewar
is one word.

priapic
from Priapus, the Roman god of male potency, is literary for highly
sexed or over-sexed:

> The famously priapic Russell (three wives, eight children).
>> (*Guardian*)

But priapic is also misused as a variation word for male sexual activity
in general:

> The pills had a priapic side-effect.
>> (Zadie Smith)

He never shied from relating his priapic endeavours.

(obituary of Milton Berle)

pricey
not pricy

primeval
not primaeval

principal, principle
these are constantly confused:

> Principle carers (as lone parents are so non-judgmentally known).
>
> (*Guardian*)

Principal as an adjective means main (the principal reason) and as a noun means the person in charge of something (the college principal); a principle is the basis of something (a principle of good education). As a college teacher once put it, 'The principal is a pal.'

prior *see* **previous, prior to**

pristine
which once meant original, ancient, primitive, is now a vogue word meaning clean, unspoilt, unused, even innocent.

clean:

> Well, the lavatories were not exactly pristine.
>
> (*Times*)

> In his pristine workshop, he shows me a 'Snob special', an old Harley Davidson completely restored.
>
> (*Daily Mail*)

unspoilt:

> In the early 1990s ... divers and tourism entrepreneurs began

showing a keen interest in what Bikini's pristine environment
and lagoon had to offer.

(Jack Niedenthal)

Buy a summer home by a pristine Scandinavian lake ...
Wooden lakeside cottages in pristine countryside.

(Sunday Times property section)

unused:

The pristine ashtray full of paperclips.

(Margaret Jull Costa, translator)

Her husband still sat in the upstairs office, at the pristine desk
topped with pockmarked red leather on which no papers lay.

(Zina Rohan)

innocent:

Self-justifying platitudes are not the appropriate tone for
Ward's replacement, however pristine.

(Mary Riddell of the Observer on John Ward, archbishop of Cardiff,
and his successor who defended the church over sex abuse of
children)

pristinely

if pristine is overused, pristinely is a monstrosity that shouldn't be used
at all:

However, British sellers may find that their peer-group buyers
are less interested in the pristinely renovated Italian villa than
the elusive wreck.

(Times)

privy council

but privy counsellor

proactive

is ugly jargon for taking the initiative (as opposed to reactive),
particularly common in business contexts.

probative
is literary for providing proof:

> They weren't probative of anything.
> (Adam Nossiter)

pro bono (publico)
(of a lawyer) is working without a fee. Hence 'his pro bono project', used about the celebrity chef Jamie Oliver's cooperative restaurant for unemployed young people.

proboscis
is literary for nose.

procrastinate *see* **prevaricate, procrastinate**

professional
the adjective professional can have a positive implication (professional preparation) or a negative one (professional foul).

progeny
is literary for children but can't be used in the singular so the following is nonsense:

> I thought we should invest in a three-wheeler for our next progeny.
> (*Guardian*)

program(me)
use programme for all non-computer uses, program for computers.

prone
(lying face downwards) is confused with supine (lying face upwards):

> Gerald White was in a 'prone position in a barber's chair, head thrown back'.
> (*Guardian*)

pronoun avoidance
is a special case of **variation**:

> Barmby also denied Boateng's claims that the Middlesbrough
> midfield player apologised afterwards.
>
> (*Times*)

How many people are referred to here? In fact Boateng and 'the
Middlesbrough player' are the same person. 'He' would be shorter and
clearer.

propeller
not propellor

prophecy, prophesy
prophecy is the noun, prophesy the verb.

pros and cons
no apostrophes needed.

proscribe *see* prescribe, proscribe

prostrate
means lying face downwards in a submissive way. See **prone**.

protagonist
a protagonist was originally the (one and only) chief actor in a drama,
and the word is still used in this sense:

> Both [dramatists] were public men whose protagonists were
> passionate about their causes.
>
> (*Guardian*)

> The show with the notoriously thin protagonist [Ally
> McBeal] was part of an extraordinarily fat decade in US telly.
>
> (*Guardian*)

But the word is also loosely used to mean participant:

Eruptions of religious boycott fever that leave the protagonists looking more idiotic than before.

(Guardian)

It is used of a contest or conflict between two people:

Saturday's protagonists [Lennox Lewis and Mike Tyson] had 71 years on the clock between them.

(Daily Telegraph)

A feud between houseboat owners ended when one of the protagonists set fire to his rival's mooring ropes.

(Daily Telegraph)

Sometimes the word chief or main is added:

The main protagonists all gave testimony.

(Guardian)

The charge against Dr Williams involves a number of evangelical groups but the chief protagonists include the Calvinist 167-year-old Church Society and Reform.

(Guardian)

Protagonist often means supporter of a particular cause:

Empire has often fostered nationalism among its protagonists and victims.

(Linda Colley, London Review of Books)

Newspapers like the New York Times were protagonists of a persecution against the church.

(Catholic cardinal)

So what is to be done? Kingsley Amis had a simple answer: 'My advice is never to say or write protagonist yourself, thereby avoiding any possible misunderstanding or obloquy on the point. If you mean a central figure, say central figure; if you mean a proponent or champion, say proponent or champion.' Agreed (though there is less room for confusion in references to drama).

protégé(e)
needs two acute accents.

protest
without at or against after it is a positive statement: to protest your innocence is to claim that you are innocent. In the US at and against are not used: you protest a decision you disagree with.

protester
not protestor

proverbial
as in 'the proverbial stitch in time' is a lame attempt to forestall criticism for using a cliché. Have the proverbial courage of your convictions: if you decide to use a cliché, go ahead without apology.

proves the rule *see* exception proves the rule

provisos
not provisoes

p's and q's
(as in mind your p's and q's) still needs apostrophes unless typography makes the distinction clear: Ps and Qs/*p*s and *q*s are alternatives.

psych, psyche
psyche is soul, spirit, mind; for slang abbreviations use psych, eg ed psych.

publicly
not publically

pulchritude
is literary for beauty.

punctilious

has just the one l. Alan Rusbridger, who edits the *Guardian*, wrote in his own paper celebrating his 'punctillious' subeditors: where were they when they were needed?

purchase

is literary for buy.

put, putt

for golf use putt; in all other cases (eg putting the shot) use put:

> He puts the shot.

pyjamas

not pajamas, which is American

pyrrhic

not Pyrrhic. A pyrrhic victory is one won at great cost (from Pyrrhus's defeat of the Romans in 279 BC) not an undecided outcome so the following is nonsense:

> But only a Pyrrhic victory is available for his team now – a draw – and even that requires a couple of monumental innings.

> (*Observer*)

Q

qua

is literary for 'as' meaning 'in the capacity, character or role of' (money qua money can't buy me love). As Burchfield notes: 'As is often the better choice of word qua word.'

quaff

is literary for both drink and drink in large draughts:

> A jolly stout man quaffing a beer.
> (Adam Nossiter)

How fast was he drinking?

quantitative

not quantitive, quantative

quash

is a technical term for annul, used in legal proceedings (the verdict was quashed). In other contexts use squash, crush (a squashed tomato, the rebellion was crushed).

Queen's, Queens'

the Oxford college is Queen's (founded by one queen); the Cambridge college is Queens' (founded by two).

queer

is now used by some gay people to refer to themselves:

Here's a piece about a group of drag artists, Duckie: 'None of it is particularly gay, but it's all very queer – in any sense of the word.'

(Rupert Smith, *Guardian*)

But use with care.

question, beg the
traditionally to beg the question means to base a logical conclusion on something that cannot be taken for granted. 'He can't be English because the English are always polite' begs the question because it assumes that English people are always polite. The expression continues to be used in this way by philosophers – but not by many other people.

To beg the question is used to mean to avoid giving a straight answer to a question and also to raise the question. This is now its most common meaning:

The case of a child psychotherapist prosecuted for sexual assault then acquitted begs questions about CPS strategy.

(*Times*)

Reading is as singular and intimate a medium as can be. Which begs the question: if the people who join book groups hate reading so much, why not be honest about it?

(*Guardian*)

Advice: for raise and avoid the question use raise and avoid, not beg. Use beg the question in its traditional sense only if you are confident your readers will understand you.

question, leading *see* leading question

question mark
a direct question should always be followed by a question mark, even when the question is rhetorical and no answer is expected.

queuing
not queueing

quite

has several contrasting meanings: quite good means less than good; quite excellent means as excellent as possible – in other words, very (this usage is particularly common in the US). And as a response 'Quite' means exactly. Be careful of confusion. *See also*: **literally**.

quixotic

no cap (from Don Quixote in Cervantes' novel) means extravagantly romantic in ideals or chivalrous in action, not eccentric, freakish, disordered.

quote

is increasingly used instead of quotation (it's a quote from Shakespeare), though some people find this usage too informal.

quotidian

is literary for daily:

> The episodes of horror become almost quotidian.
> (*Guardian*)

R

raccoon

not racoon

race

is used in biology to refer to animals, plants and micro-organisms and it was once a common alternative to people, nation or community (the English/British race). But this usage is oldfashioned and could be offensive. Use people, nation or community.

racism, racist

not racialism, racialist; this is simply a matter of style: there is no difference in meaning.

rack

not wrack in the following: rack and ruin, rack your brains, racked with pain. Wrack is seaweed.

racket

not racquet in tennis and squash, as well as for noise, swindle etc

racy

not racey

raise, rise

children are now raised in Britain as in the US, but a British salary increase remains a rise not a raise.

Ralegh

not Raleigh, is the recommended spelling for Sir Walter, the Elizabethan soldier, explorer and writer.

Range Rover

doesn't have a hyphen but Land-Rover does.

rarebit *see* **welsh rabbit, rarebit**

raspberry *see* **rhyming slang**

rateable

not ratable

ravage, ravish

to ravage is to devastate, lay waste, destroy (the invading troops ravaged the countryside); to ravish can be to rape, but also to enchant, enrapture, entrance – hence the adjective ravishing, which means delightful (the visitors found the countryside ravishing). Use these words with care.

raze

not rase; to raze is to demolish so 'to the ground' after it is always redundant:

> The house had been razed to the ground.
> *(Times)*

razzmatazz

is the recommended spelling.

re, re-

most compound verbs with the prefix re (again) do not need a hyphen. But hyphens are used to avoid confusion between two different words (re-creation, the remaking of something, as opposed to recreation, amusement) and to avoid an ugly repetition of the letter e (re-enact as opposed to reenact).

realise

not realize

realpolitik

practical politics based on realities rather than principles: no cap.

reason is because

this expression is a clear case of redundancy:

> The reason Britain went to war is because the Americans
> asked for their support.

This should be either 'The reason Britain went to war is that the
Americans ...' or 'Britain went to war because the Americans ...'

reason why

why is redundant after the reason:

> The reason why Britain went to war was to support the US.

Omit why. One reason this expression seems so familiar may be that
Tennyson's poem 'The Charge of the Light Brigade' includes the line
(punctuated as in the original):

> Their's not to reason why.

But Tennyson was using reason as a verb meaning to think.

rebarbative

is literary for repellent:

> Then it seemed to me my body was simply the terrain for a
> rebarbative courtship.

> (Zina Rohan)

rebut, refute

refute is more common than rebut but these words present essentially
the same problem. They have a traditional meaning, still insisted on by

usage guides and style books, and a popular use which is very different. Both rebut and refute are used by most people to mean deny:

rebut:

Once the press is in a foaming frenzy, rebuttals only make matters worse.

(Polly Toynbee, *Guardian*)

ENO quickly rebutted the rumours.
(*Guardian*)

refute:

Her relationship with Sir William broke down after she spent yesterday refuting his claims that she tried to influence the inquiry.

(*Guardian*)

He would never refute the beauty of her singing.
(Ann Patchett)

But traditionally to rebut a statement or claim means much more than deny: it means to offer clear evidence or reasoned argument against it:

A potentially devastating rebuttal of the government's persistent claim has emerged from a new study.

(*Private Eye*)

And to refute a statement or claim goes further: it means to disprove it:

An insinuation at once infuriating and impossible to refute.
(Jonathan Frantzen)

I refute it *thus*.
(Dr Johnson of Bishop Berkeley's theory of the non-existence of matter as he kicked a stone)

Even among literate and literary people there is confusion over rebut and refute. Here the two words seem to be treated as equivalent:

> Frayn attempts to rebut Paul Lawrence Rose's description of Copenhagen [a play] as possessing 'a subtle revisionism' ... Frayn fails to refute Rose.
>
> (Tom Paulin in a letter to the *Guardian*)

Advice: in ordinary writing it is better to do without these words. They can confuse everybody and are liable to irritate some people when their use is considered incorrect.

reconciled to
not with

recur
not reoccur

redundancy *see* **tautology**

referendums
not referenda

reflection
not reflexion

refulgent
is literary for radiant:

> They knew he was a small, obsessive, honest character entirely lacking in refulgence.
>
> (Hugo Young on Iain Duncan Smith, *Guardian*)

regalia
means royal insignia so 'royal regalia' is ridiculous.

regime
has no accent.

register

not registry office for weddings

regretful, regrettable

regretful means showing regret; regrettable means causing it (his conduct was regrettable and he is now regretful).

regularly

is often used to mean often:

> And is there any mystery in rugby more wonderfully puzzling than the question of how France can turn themselves around so brilliantly, so regularly, to play a game like this?
>
> *(Sunday Times)*

> Americans plead it [the fifth amendment] regularly, thus effectively incriminating themselves.
>
> (Matthew Engel, *Guardian*)

But regularly is also used to mean at regular intervals:

> We have a seven-year-old daughter who sees her father regularly.
>
> *(Guardian* problem page letter)

So which is this?

> The only sport regularly to change its rules is rugby.
>
> (Simon Jenkins, *Times*)

reiterate

is literary for repeat and repeat again.

relative, relation

are both used for people in family relationships. The two words mean the same thing but as Longman notes: 'For some reason we speak of rich or poor relations but of elderly relatives.' Also contrasted with rich relations are wealthy relatives. Wealthy, elderly and relative belong in the same box: prefer relations, rich or poor.

relatively *see* **comparatively, relatively**

remission
used in a medical context can confuse patients and their well-wishers. Its primary medical definition is a lessening in the degree or intensity of an illness. Thus a cancer is in remission if the patient's condition has improved. But 'being in remission' is also used to stress that the patient's improvement is temporary:

> 'It's marvellous that Sybil is getting better,' he said ... 'No – she's in remission,' he said flatly. 'Her doctor told me it often happens.'
>
> (Elizabeth Jane Howard)

renaissance
not renascence for rebirth, revival

rendezvous
is one word.

repel, repulse
are both used to mean drive back (the Gauls repelled/repulsed the Roman invaders); repulse is the stronger word and more common in this context. Repel is also used to mean disgust (his behaviour repelled me). Disgusting behaviour is repellent or repulsive (again the stronger word), but things like fabrics and creams can only be repellent, as in water-repellent and insect-repellent.

repellent
not repellant. See **repel, repulse**.

repertoire, repertory
a repertoire is the list of items that a person or company can perform; a repertory company is a theatre company with a repertoire of plays.

repetition

English is full of repetitive phrases like pomp and ceremony, neat and tidy, whys and wherefores. The law, aiming to be comprehensive, provides examples like aid and abet, by let or hindrance, the rest, residue and remainder. These phrases trip off the tongue but you should avoid them in ordinary writing. *See also*: **variation**.

repine

is literary for fret, complain.

replete

is literary for full.

restaurateur

is spelt like this: there is no n in it.

restructuring *see* euphemism

résumé

summary (and in the US, curriculum vitae) has two acute accents; resume means to start again.

resuscitation

a difficult word to spell and highly charged. Its general meaning is the urgent medical treatment needed when someone's life is in immediate danger, from a condition that has arisen either suddenly (eg from a severe allergic reaction) or gradually (eg collapse occurring because of dehydration on a very hot day).

But resuscitation also has a specific meaning in the term cardiopulmonary resuscitation (CPR), which is the urgent action taken when the heart stops. This has become a highly charged issue because of 'do not resuscitate' (DNR) orders and the question of who (doctors, patients, relatives) should be involved in making these orders. Note that DNR does not mean 'do not *treat*', only 'do not try to restart the heart if it stops'.

reticent

is used to mean reserved, reluctant to speak – and reluctant to act in general. The second usage, a French import, is growing. After Katharine Hepburn's death in 2003, her *Guardian* obituary included an example of the traditional usage, reserved:

She mixed profound reticence with abrupt surges of out-spokenness.

The same edition of the paper included an example of reticence meaning reluctance in general:

> Selznick's reticence to let her play Scarlett [O'Hara in *Gone With The Wind*] referred pretty obviously to her body.
>
> (Zadie Smith)

As reticence is used to mean reluctance, phrases like 'reticent to talk' are becoming common:

> Men are more reticent to talk about their diseases.
>
> (surgeon quoted by Libby Brooks, *Guardian*)

> Until now, I have been reticent about talking about anti-semitism.
>
> (Jonathan Sacks, *Guardian*)

> Southwell was wary and reticent to speak on the record.
>
> (*Brisbane Courier-Mail*)

Prefer reluctant for things in general; and be careful of using reticent to mean reserved since some people may not get the message.

reverend, reverent
reverend means deserving reverence and is used as a title for clergymen, eg the Rev(erend) John Smith. The Rev J Smith and the Rev Mr/Dr Smith are also possible but (the) Rev Smith is a mistake. Reverent means showing reverence.

revert back
to revert is to go back so back after it is redundant.

review, revue
a revue is a light theatrical entertainment; a review is a critical notice (she wrote a favourable review of the revue).

rhetorical adverbs

modern English, particularly journalism and advertising, uses a lot of rhetorical adverbs, words intended to grab the reader's attention without having too much meaning. Examples are: actually, always, definitely, invariably, literally, really, regularly, routinely, truly, uniquely, virtually. Some writers stick words like almost in front of them to try to give them meaning as well as impact. This doesn't work. *See also*: **actually**; **invariably**; **literally**; **regularly**; **routinely**.

rhyme

not rime for the poetic device (but *The Rime of the Ancient Mariner*); rime is frost.

rhyming slang

is routine in working-class speech, particularly in the London area, and some expressions are now part of mainstream English. To have a butcher's (hook) is to look; to use your loaf (of bread) is to use your head; to rabbit (and pork) is to talk; to tell porkies (pork pies) is to lie; to scarper (Scapa Flow) is to go; on your tod (from Tod Sloan, an American jockey) is on your own.

Then there are the euphemisms for body parts and functions, used by some people in ignorance of their origin:

berk (Berkeley hunt): cunt
bottle (and glass): arse, so courage; also aris(totle) for bottle
bristols (City): titty
cobbler's (awls): balls
raspberry (tart): fart
wick (as in get on my): dick, prick

riffle, rifle

these two are easily confused. To riffle through, eg the pages of a book, is to make a casual search; to rifle (sometimes with through) is to ransack. You would rifle not riffle a cashbox:

Molly used to have a cashbox but Elsie riffled it.
(Gloria Emerson)

rigor, rigour
rigor is muscular rigidity (rigor mortis); rigour is strictness, hardness etc (the rigours of army life).

Riley, the life of
not Reilly

rime *see* rhyme

rise *see* raise, rise

rites of passage
not rights, for ceremonies marking a person's change of status, eg from youth to adult

roach
is a coy American abbreviation of cockroach; also (the butt of) a marijuana cigarette.

rock'n'roll
has two apostrophes.

role
has no accent.

Rolls-Royce
has a hyphen.

Romania
not Roumania, Rumania

rooster
is an American euphemism for cock (male bird).

roué
needs an acute accent.

routinely
like regularly, is rhetorical for often.

Royal Botanic Gardens at Kew
not Botanical

royal family
no caps

rule, exception that proves the *see* **exception proves the rule**

russian roulette
no caps

S

s

the letter s is sometimes added before a vowel but not a consonant (antiques expert but antique shop, dealer; features editor but feature writer) in writing as in speech. To add the s before the consonant is not wrong but unnecessary.

saccharin, saccharine

saccharin is a substitute for sugar; saccharine means sugary, both literally and metaphorically.

sacrilegious

not sacreligious; the word, which comes from sacred, has nothing to do with religion.

safe *see* haven

Sahara desert

strictly speaking, there should be no desert here since the word sahara is Arabic for desert.

St Thomas's hospital

in London, needs the s after the apostrophe since it is sounded in speech (although the hospital itself doesn't use it).

saleable

not salable

salon, saloon

a salon is a French living or reception room, particularly a grand one, a social gathering (eg of writers) in such a room and the place where hairdressers and beauticians operate. A saloon is a public room on a ship and a bar in the US, particularly in westerns. In Britain the saloon (or lounge) bar is the comfortable alternative to the public bar and a saloon car is an oldfashioned term for an enclosed one.

salubrious, salutary, sanitary

all refer to health but are used differently. Salubrious is literary for healthy and pleasant to live in (a salubrious district); salutary is mainly metaphorical and means beneficial (he learnt a salutary lesson); sanitary is used of cleanliness, freedom from infection and public health, and specifically of drainage and sewage disposal; also of sanitary towels etc used by women during menstruation.

salvoes

is the plural of salvo meaning a volley of shots but salvos is the plural of the (less common) word salvo meaning reason or excuse.

sanatorium

not sanitarium, sanitorium, for room or building for sick people

sanction

the dominant sense of sanction as a noun is economic action taken by one or more states against another state (the UN imposed sanctions on Iraq). Another, less common and almost opposite, meaning is official approval (the US and Britain sought UN sanction for their war against Iraq). Confusingly, sanction as a verb usually means authorise (her parents sanctioned the marriage) but occasionally impose sanctions on, penalise (he was sanctioned for his behaviour).

Advice: use sanction as a noun to mean action against not approval; to avoid confusion don't use sanction as a verb.

sangfroid

coolness, self-possession, is one word.

sarcasm

a sarcastic remark is a sneer intended to cause pain or at least discomfort. It is usually ironical; that is, the words used have a different meaning from their surface one: 'Looking for something?' to somebody who has just tripped and fallen over. Keep the word sarcasm for sneers which have a suggestion of irony. *See also*: **irony.**

sari, sarong

sari not saree for the Hindu woman's traditional body-covering garment; a sarong is a length of cloth worn as a skirt by men and women in Malaysia and Polynesia, and now a western woman's light dress, particularly for the beach (also worn by David Beckham).

sauternes

a sweet white wine, comes from the district of Sauternes, a village south of Bordeaux.

savannah

not savanna for tropical grassland. Savannah in Georgia (and Tennessee) has the h although Americans prefer savanna for grassland.

save

is literary for except (they were all rescued save one).

scallop, escalope

scallop not scollop or escallop for the shellfish, shallow pan or dish, decorative edging; an escalope is a thin, boneless slice of meat, particularly veal.

scan

can mean either glance at (he scanned the football results as they ate) or examine carefully (he scanned the document several times); it also means (of verse) to conform with the rules of metre (this line doesn't scan). Use with care.

scare quotes

are quote marks used round slang or clichés to distance the writer from the expression (some 'cowboys' failed to fix my roof). To be avoided unless you wish to give the impression of being a fussy academic writer.

scarves
is the plural of scarf.

schadenfreude
no caps or italics, is pleasure in the misfortune of others.

schizophrenia, schizophrenic
schizophrenia is a psychotic mental illness marked by delusions. The adjective schizophrenic is sometimes used to disparage people and organisations said to show contradictory tendencies (the local authority was accused of a schizophrenic approach to education) but this usage is considered offensive and should be avoided.

Scotch, Scots, Scottish
Scotch (a contraction of Scottish) was once used as an ordinary adjective by the people of Scotland (eg by Burns, Scott and the great dictionary-maker James Murray writing in 1866) to refer to themselves, and it is still universally used for things like scotch broth, egg, mist and whisky. And Burchfield quotes a language expert writing in 1992 as saying: 'For working class Scots the common form has long been Scotch ... and the native form Scots is sometimes regarded as an Anglicised affectation.'

By contrast many middle-class Scots consider Scotch to be an insult. One wrote to the *Guardian* in 2003: 'This word, whatever its 19th century usage, now bears the same relationship to Scotsman as "Paki" does to Pakistani.'

So, to avoid offending anybody, use the long form Scottish as the adjective.

scourge
(whip) is confused with bugbear:

> [Benny] Hill, the latter-day scourge of feminism, whose
> original success coincided with the advent of television.
>
> (*Observer*)

Benny Hill had no interest in whipping feminists: it was they who wanted to whip him.

screamers
that's to say exclamation marks, should be used rarely.

scrutiny
close before scrutiny is redundant since to scrutinise is to examine carefully.

sea change
two words. This is an irrelevant allusion (in almost every case) to Ariel's song in *The Tempest*:

> Full fathom five thy father lies;
> Of his bones are coral made:
> Those are pearls that were his eyes:
> Nothing of him that doth fade,
> But doth suffer a sea-change
> Into something rich and strange.

Elizabeth Jane Howard called one of her novels *The Sea Change*; avoid.

seafood
is a picturesque word which can mean either shellfish by itself or fish and shellfish taken together. Where precision is important (discussion of allergies, religious taboos, health benefits etc) prefer fish and/or shellfish.

seasonable, seasonal
seasonable means appropriate to the season so 'seasonable weather' is snow in winter, sun in summer. Seasonal is a more general adjective meaning in season, characteristic of the seasons or a particular one, so 'seasonal work' is work available at a particular time of year.

second *see* first and second

second biggest *see* after

secondhand

is one word except in cases like the second hand (of a secondhand watch).

second world war *see* world war

self–

compound words formed with self should be hyphenated. In 'self-censoring yourself' yourself is redundant; in 'a self-confessed murderer' self is redundant.

Sellotape

is a trade name. Except when referring to this brand use sticky tape.

seminal

(from *semen*, Latin for seed) is used in a metaphorical sense to mean original and influential and it still has a literal meaning (eg seminal fluid). When the metaphor is used in a sexual context, the effect is unfortunate, whether or not the writer knows what they're doing. (In this case, clearly, they do.)

> My mind raced back in time to poor Ron Davies and his famous moment of madness on Clapham Common. It was a seminal moment for me, too: it was when I first noticed this same radical change in this country.
>
> (Minette Marrin, *Sunday Times*)

Semitic

the Semitic peoples include the Arabs and others as well as the Jews but anti-semitic normally means just anti-Jewish.

sensual, sensuous

there is total confusion in the use of these words. Milton is said to have coined sensuous to mean relating to the senses in general as opposed to sensual, which implied physical, usually sexual, gratification. But the two words now seem interchangeable.

First here's sensuous used in the Miltonic sense:

Computer or television images literalise things. They rob objects of their sensuous presence.

(Bryan Appleyard, *Sunday Times*)

The morbid introspective Picasso, and the colourful sensuous joie de vivre of Matisse.

(*Guardian*)

But sensual is used in the same non-sexual way:

Flowers ... the sensual pleasure we take in them.
(Michael Pollan)

There must be plenty of Keats, for those moments of wallowing intensity and sensual enjoyment of language.

(Michael Binyon, *Times*)

Another of my favourite places is Morocco, because it's very French and so sensual. The music, the smells, the colours – it's just this feast of sensations that leaves you feeling somehow enriched.

(Petula Clark interviewed in the *Sunday Times*)

In the same way both sensual and sensuous are used to suggest sex:

sensual:

The performance of Meat Joy involves scantily clad young men and women engaging in a kind of art-orgy, sensually painting one another's bodies and rolling about with raw meat.

By sticking to the most expensive and sensual fabrics, the C&L [cashmere and leather] woman is making an unmissable statement about her husband's salary, his potency, the fabulous quality of their sex life.

sensuous:

> The mixture of religious metaphors and sensuous love is as old as John Donne.

> A sensuous tongue-and-mouth massage in a secret sex parlour.

The two words even turn up in successive sentences – referring to the same old thing:

> You can be sensuous, erotic, without being dirty. It's nothing to do with dirt, it's to do with sensuality.
>
> (Guardian – like the four quotes above)

In some cases context makes the meaning clear; in others confusion remains. What does sensuality mean here?

> Freud is more interested in beauty than he is in cruelty. So many paintings are devoted to a hunt for elusive moments of sensuality and delicacy.
>
> (Waldemar Januszczak, Sunday Times)

Advice: never use sensual in the Miltonic sense or sensuous in the sexual sense; where precision is essential (eg a lonely hearts ad) avoid them both.

sentence adverbs

are those like presumably, thankfully and hopefully which refer to the sentence as a whole (presumably, he'll be at the meeting). Other examples are frankly, simply, inevitably, happily, thankfully, mercifully. A difficulty with some sentence adverbs is that they can also be used to refer to part of a sentence (they were happily married as opposed to happily, they were married). See **hopefully**.

sentences

should not be too long and rambling:

> I can't speak for the band members, except to suggest that as musicians during their formative years, alcohol, and possibly other substances (unless they are the only three musicians from that period who, by some minor miracle, steered clear of the

temptation) would probably have featured in one way or another, which could explain why Dave Temple's interpretation of blues numbers from the 1920s, 30s and 40s was among the finest I've heard.

(anonymous music review, *French News*)

sergeant, serjeant
sergeant is the ordinary word used in the army and police, but the old spelling serjeant is still used in legal and ceremonial contexts.

serial, series
a serial is a novel or drama, published/broadcast/shown in instalments; a series is a number of successive programmes featuring the same character(s).

serial comma
the serial comma (also called the Oxford comma because it is the house style of the Oxford University Press) is the second comma in 'His downfall was wine, women, and song'. It's pointless in routine lists so leave it out. But include it where necessary for clarity as in 'The menu was steak, fish and chips, and omelette'.

serviette *see* napkin, serviette and u/non-u

several
usually means more than three, a few.

sewage, sewer, sewerage
sewage is waste; sewerage is the system of sewers which disposes of it.

sex *see* gender

sexist language
it's difficult to believe that in the 1970s a book for trainee journalists could be published in Britain under the title *Newsman's English*. It was by the then editor of the *Sunday Times* Harold Evans who had the reputation of being an innovative, even radical, journalist. Other terms used in the book were newspaperman and deskman (for subeditor).

In the past 30 years there has been a noticeable shift away from terms like fireman towards non-sexist alternatives like firefighter. This is for two connected reasons: more women now do jobs that were traditionally men's so the old terms are inaccurate; and there has been strong pressure from feminists to abandon them. They haven't disappeared but they are on their way out.

See also **feminine forms** for discussion of words like actress, **he/she, s/he, he or she** and **-person**.

Shakespeare, Shakespearian
are the recommended spellings.

shall, will
there is a traditional distinction between shall and will with one expressing the simple future and the other determination or obligation. I/we shall is the simple future while I/will suggests determination (it may be difficult but I will do it). With you, he, she, it and they it's the other way round: you will is the simple future; you shall suggests obligation or the speaker's determination (you may not want to do it but you shall).

But so few speakers and writers make the distinction that it is, for practical purposes, obsolete. Shall I/we survives in questions (shall I phone for a taxi?) but otherwise will (or 'll) is the common form.

shambles
a slaughterhouse, so a bloody mess, so a mess (your bedroom is a shambles). A tired metaphor, a cliché, but not a crime.

she/her *see* I/me

shew *see* show

sheikh
not sheik

show
not shew

Siam, Siamese
use Thailand, Thai, except for Siamese cat. Prefer conjoined twins to Siamese twins.

sic

is Latin for so. In square brackets after a quoted word [sic], it means that this is exactly what the quoted person said/wrote.

sick, ill

both words mean in bad health in British English but the dominant meaning of to be sick is to vomit and to feel sick is to feel like vomiting. To be ill is to have an illness but 'I was ill on the ferry' is a euphemistic way of saying 'I was sick on the ferry.' At the same time there are numerous current expressions in which sick means ill: off sick, sick leave, sick note, sick pay etc. The injury-prone footballer Darren Anderton was nicknamed Sicknote.

silicon, silicone

silicon is a chemical element used in electrical components (silicon chip and Silicon Valley); silicone is a derivative of silicon used as a lubricant, an adhesive and a breast implant.

simile *see* **metaphor, simile**

simply

is one of those adverbs that rarely does anything useful:

> It [Lonnie Donegan's 'Rock Island Line'] had a vitality, a rhythmic intensity and an earthy simplicity that – at the time – was simply unique in British pop.
>
> (*Guardian*)

singeing, singing

singeing is burning; singing is giving tongue.

singulars and plurals *see* **number agreement**

situation

avoid expressions like crisis situation (we realised we were in a crisis situation) which can mean no more than a crisis for the verbose.

sizeable

not sizable

skeleton in the closet/cupboard

traditionally, a secret source of discredit, pain or shame can be a skeleton in either the closet or the cupboard. But since the closet is now particularly used of gays who have not come out, 'skeleton in the closet' may be misunderstood:

> PG Wodehouse, Noël Coward and Charlie Chaplin. All had skeletons in their closets.
>
> (Robert Harris, *Daily Telegraph*)

Harris does not want to imply that all three were gay but a reader might get this idea. Prefer cupboard to closet for skeletons.

skier, skyer

a skier is one who skis on snow (or water); a skyer is a ball hit high into the air.

skiing

not ski-ing

slander *see* libel, slander

slang

is the essence of colloquial speech and so should not be used in formal writing. The problem is not the definition but how to apply it since the slang of yesterday can be the standard English of today. The word mob, for example, was once slang. Bimbo and couch potato are cited by Burchfield as examples of modern slang but neither would raise an eyebrow if used in a broadsheet newspaper. *See also*: **rhyming slang**.

slate

to slate is to criticise strongly (the critic slated the play). Be careful if your reader is American since in the US to slate can be to schedule or designate (the play was slated for Broadway).

sleep with

as a euphemism for having sex is out of date and in some contexts ridiculous:

> [Guy] Burgess is the most prolific sexual athlete I've ever

come across. He's rampantly sexual and spends half his time in toilets in Hyde Park sleeping with everybody and anyone.

(Peter Moffat, quoted by Smallweed in the *Guardian*)

smelt
not smelled; a smelt is also a small fish.

smidgen
not smidgin, smidgeon

smoky
not smokey

snuck
is American for sneaked.

sobriquet
not soubriquet, is literary (and posh) for nickname:

> Mrs [Posh] Beckham – who was thought to dislike her Spice Girl sobriquet.
>
> (*Times*)

soi-disant
is literary for self-styled; it does not mean so-called.

some
is literary for about (there were some 200 people there).

somewhat
is literary (and American) for rather (I am somewhat indisposed).

South, Latin America
these are not the same thing at all. South America does not include Central America; Latin America consists of South America, Central America and Mexico.

speciality

not specialty for the thing a person specialises in (the chef's speciality is roast veal); specialty is the American form of speciality and also has the technical meaning of a contract under seal.

spelt

not spelled

spicy

not spicey

spiky

not spikey

spilt

not spilled

split infinitive

there's no such thing. This was the technical view of the grammarian Otto Jespersen in 1933, endorsed by Trask in 2001. Their argument is that the preposition 'to' does not form part of the infinitive, so 'to boldly go' is not a split infinitive because the infinitive is 'go' not 'to go'. In support of this argument is the point that the infinitive doesn't necessarily have 'to' in front of it. 'I asked him to go' and 'He made me go' are both examples of the infinitive.

Language experts insist that whatever it's called, the 'split infinitive' is not a grammatical mistake. The writer Stephen Leacock (quoted by David Crystal) pointed out that many verbs 'are themselves split infinitives, as when we say to undertake or to overthrow'.

In the same way an adverb–verb combination can be so common and familiar that it becomes an expression in its own right, as with sexually harass, verbally abuse – and in the words of the song, accidentally fall:

> In a World Cup in which potential champions have been acting like 10 green bottles, Italy managed by a whisker to miss their turn to accidentally fall last night.
>
> (Simon Barnes, *Times*)

Accidentally to fall and to fall accidentally wouldn't quite work. That said, there is a problem with splitting infinitives. Some readers are prejudiced against them and they can be clumsy and awkward:

> Latimer said: 'I am relieved to hopefully find that the world will believe I did not hop into bed with John Major.'
>
> (*Sunday Times*)

> I always feel I get enough stimulation at work, without rushing off to frantically do sights in 48 hours.
>
> (Nicholas Coleridge quoted by the *Sunday Times*)

But attempts to avoid splitting infinitives can be clumsy and awkward too:

> If only in order properly to chart that ocean, however, historians need to move beyond nationalist pieties and preoccupations.
>
> (Linda Colley, *London Review of Books*)

> He was said regularly to have given verbal permission to slaughter animals.
>
> (Robert Gildea)

There's another problem in the second example where 'regularly' seems at first to refer to 'said'. And in the next example 'secretly' could refer to 'instructs' or 'develop':

> He instructs his scientists secretly to develop weapons of mass destruction.
>
> (John Sutherland, *Guardian*)

It's clear that putting the adverb before the infinitive, to avoid splitting it, is usually awkward and sometimes confusing. General advice on splitting and not-splitting: first check if the adverb is essential; cut it if you can. Then see if putting the adverb after the infinitive would make the sentence read better and still be clear.

If not, carry on splitting. You will be in the company of writers like Coleridge, Donne, George Eliot and George Bernard Shaw, who was a passionate defender of the right to boldly split.

spoilt
not spoiled

spoonfuls
not spoonsful or spoons full

square brackets
(as opposed to round ones) have a particular function: to show that something has been added to a quoted passage by the writer, editor or whatever:

> He [the hero] dies in the end.

stadiums
not stadia

stagy
not stagey

stalactites, stalagmites
are cave deposits of calcium carbonate; stalactites hang down; stalagmites stick up.

stanch, staunch
to stanch is to stop the flow of something, eg blood ; staunch is loyal.

standard English
is criticised by some academic language experts on the grounds that no one version of a language can be superior to another. Trask concedes this point ('Standard English is not more beautiful or more logical than other varieties of English') but then explains why it is necessary to have a standard:

> It is simply *convenient* to have a standard form of the language which is agreed on by everybody ... Like a standard electrical plug, like a standard videotape, like a standard size for car tyres, standard English is valuable because it *is* standardised.

Trask then makes the point that recognised varieties of standard

English have developed for different purposes, eg scientific research and arts criticism. And of course academic writing in general. However hostile the language experts may be to standard English they always write in it rather than in scouse, say, or cockney – which rather weakens their case.

stationary, stationery
stationary is an adjective meaning not moving; stationery is writing materials, so a stationery van would be full of things like paper and envelopes.

staunch *see* stanch, staunch

stellar
which means starlike, is literary for impressive:

> Mike Golding has had to cope with the stellar presence of MacArthur.
>
> > *(Times)*

> Bigger babies do better at school, have more stellar careers.
>
> > *(Guardian)*

stepfather, stepmother
but step-parent

sterling
not stirling for the pound and the adjective meaning genuine, of good character

stile, style
stile for steps over a fence; style for the way of doing something, particularly writing.

stilettos
not stilettoes

still lifes
is the plural of still life, painting of inanimate object.

stilton cheese

no cap

stimulant, stimulus

a stimulant is a drug; a stimulus is everything else that stimulates, ie produces a response in a living organism or encourages increased activity (the fine weather was a stimulus for the builders who finished the roof quickly).

stodgy

not stodgey

stony

not stoney

storey, story

a storey is the floor level of a building; a story is a narrative. Both are story in the US.

storm

not stormy petrel

straight, strait

these words are not related though they are often confused. As an adjective straight means uncurved, direct, normal; as a noun it means the last part of a racecourse, a heterosexual etc; and as an adverb it means directly (go straight home). Strait as an adjective means narrow and as a noun a narrow place or passage, particularly at sea (the Straits of Dover), and a difficulty (dire straits).

Straightaway and straightforward come from straight; straitjacket and straitlaced from strait. To straighten means to make or become straight; to straiten is archaic for to narrow, put into difficulty and survives only in the cliché for hardship, straitened circumstances.

Strasbourg

not Strasburg, Strassburg

strata

is the plural of stratum so 'this strata' is wrong.

strike action

as in 'The union decided to take strike action' is nonsense because strike is already a very active verb. Prefer 'The union decided to strike.'

stripy

not stripey

sty

not stye both for pigs and swellings on the eye

stymie

not stimy, stymy, for obstruct, obstruction

subjunctive, the

the subjunctive mood is a form of the verb used when something is imagined, wished, demanded, suggested, insisted etc (she demanded that he come). The main contrast is with the indicative mood (because she demanded, he is coming).

Is the British subjunctive on the way out? Partridge, Bryson and Trask seem to think so but Burchfield and the Longman guide say, on the contrary, that the subjunctive is increasingly found in British English.

Be that as it may, it's not difficult to find examples of the failure to use the subjunctive, as in this letter to the *Guardian* about Charles and Di:

A prudish word in Charlie's ear suggested she wears a bra.

If the subjunctive had been used, the sentence would have read 'suggested she *wear* a bra' – and would have been clearer to those who recognise a subjunctive when they see one. The problem is that many people don't. If you have any doubts on the matter, there is another way of writing the sentence using should. It is both grammatically correct and unambiguous:

A prudish word in Charlie's ear suggested she *should wear* a bra.

The subjective or should formula is needed after words like suggest(ion), insist(ence), demand, wish, persuade, stipulate/ion, request, recommend(ation), when they are followed by a clause starting with that (or where that is understood):

> She insisted Peter sit there/should sit there.

> It was his wish that they be rewarded/should be rewarded.

A second common use of the subjunctive is in fossilised phrases like the one used above – be that as it may. Others are: so be it, perish the thought, come what may. And a third is in cases like 'As it were', 'If I were you' and 'I wish she were here.'

substitute
if in a recipe butter is replaced by margarine, margarine is substituted (is the substitute) for butter. But in football when a player is replaced by a substitute, the player on the pitch is substituted. This usage may be annoying but it is irresistible: 'David Beckham was substituted' means that he was replaced. To avoid confusion use replace instead of substitute as a verb.

sucking
not suckling pig

suffice it
(to say) is literary for let it be enough.

sufficient
is literary for enough.

suit, suite
suit for clothes, playing cards, lawsuit; suite for retinue, set of rooms: en suite means a bedroom with bathroom attached.

superlative *see* comparative, superlative

supersede

not supercede

supervisor

not superviser

surveille

which exists in American English as a back-formation from surveillance, is occasionally found in Britain:

> In those early days, when relatively few people were actually surveilled, there was only a single group of campaigners who made any fuss.
>
> (David Leigh and Richard Norton-Taylor, *Guardian*)

Not recommended: use to be under surveillance or spied on.

sustain

is formal for suffer (he sustained a broken leg) but suffer is itself literary: why not 'he broke his leg' or 'his leg was broken'?

swap

not swop

swat, swot

to swat is to hit sharply (swat that fly); to swot is to study hard.

swathe

not swath for a strip of cut grass or corn and so for a section:

> The fact that being gay is no longer an issue for huge swathes of the Establishment.
>
> (*Observer*)

swearwords *see* **four-letter words**

swingeing

to swinge is archaic for to beat but the adjective swingeing (with an e to distinguish it from swinging) meaning thumping, great, survives (swingeing increases in taxation).

swop *see* swap

syndrome

a syndrome is a group of symptoms (ie the patient's complaints) and signs (ie what the doctor finds by examination) which occur together so that it makes sense to assume that they show a particular disease process. Syndromes are often described before the cause of the disease is known.

So-called Gulf war syndrome is not generally accepted as such by doctors. Sufferers may have real physical complaints, but their symptoms are too varied between one sufferer and another for the term syndrome to apply.

synopses

is the plural of synopsis.

systematic, systemic

systematic means methodical and thorough (a systematic search); systemic means affecting the system or body as a whole (a systemic pesticide).

T

table
in Britain to table a proposal is to put it on the agenda (to bring it *to* the table) whereas in the US it's to withdraw it from the agenda indefinitely (to take it *away from* the table).

tableaux
is the plural of tableau.

table d'hôte
for set meal, should have the circumflex accent over the o, partly as a reminder that the h before it is silent.

tablespoonfuls *see* spoonfuls

tactile
has a traditional low-key, non-sexual meaning, pleasing to the touch, as in this reference to a toy train set:

> It was so indelibly tactile, the heft in the hand of loco and tender and coach.
>
> *(Times)*

and this reference to garden furniture:

> Prince Charles wanted the pieces to be sculptural and tactile.
> *(US Architectural Digest)*

It also has a trendy modern meaning:

She [Norma Major] was totally unaware of her husband's reputation in the capital for flirting and for being tactile.

(*Daily Mail*)

I danced with —. He was very tactile.
(evidence in rape case by alleged victim, *Times*)

Juan Carlos is ... a little too attentive. He is very tactile.
(Princess Diana, according to her protection officer, *Sunday Times*)

These examples are a touch coy. Here's a more explicit example:

As the drinks flowed, she became increasingly tactile – a pat on the bum in the kitchen, a stroke of the arm outside the bathroom, the rub of thigh against thigh as we sat on the sofa.

(*Sunday Times*)

To be tactile in the modern sense, then, is to touch people up.

takable
not takeable

tandem
in tandem means more than merely linked together; it means with one in front of another, as on a tandem bicycle.

target
outside archery and shooting, target seems to be losing its original meaning of something to be hit and becoming a synonym for aim or objective, so targets are achieved or reached – or exceeded, which is particularly silly. If a target isn't hittable it's not much of a target: prefer aim or objective. Target as a verb can be precise and effective: in marketing strategy certain consumers are targeted so that an advertising campaign will hit them with maximum impact. Keep target the verb for this kind of thing – aggression – rather than as a variation word for aim.

targeted, targeting
not targetted, targetting

taskforce
is one word.

tautology
is the unnecessary repetition of what has been said/is being said, eg *safe*
haven (a haven is a refuge), *free* gift (a gift is not paid for) and revert
back (to revert is to go back). Other words for this are redundancy and
pleonasm. Intentional repetition for effect is very different.

tax avoidance, evasion
they may sound similar but tax avoidance is a clever – and legal – way
of paying less tax, whereas tax evasion is only clever until you're caught
because it's illegal.

taxiing
is one word.

teaspoonfuls *see* **spoonfuls**

tee-shirt *see* **T-shirt**

Teesside, Cleveland
double s, one word

terra firma
originally this meant the mainland as opposed to islands but it is now
dry land or the ground as opposed to water or the sky.

terrorism, terrorist
these words are among the most loaded in the political vocabulary.
You say terrorist, I say freedom fighter; or vice versa. The least
emotive word to describe an irregular fighter is guerrilla, a Spanish
word in use since the Peninsular War of 1808–14. The declared policy
of Reuters, the international news agency, is: 'Prefer a neutral term
like guerrillas to terrorists.'

Since the US president George W Bush 'declared war on terrorism' in response to 11 September, it has become even more difficult to use 'terror' and its derivatives in a calm, analytical way. But, as Peter Preston, ex-editor of the *Guardian*, wrote in April 2002:

> Terror made Makarios president of Cyprus and Kenyatta president of Kenya. The terror of the Stern gang was there at the birth of Israel. Terror sits behind ministerial desks in Belfast and lurks in the antechambers of Islamabad. This terror [in the Middle East] is not uniquely evil. Terror is a known and tacitly accepted means to regional or national end.

And it's worth adding that the first 'terrorists' were not ashamed to use the term about themselves. They were the Jacobins in the French revolution who used the power of the state – and the guillotine – as instruments of democracy.

than I/me

which should it be? 'He is taller than I' or 'He is taller than me'? Traditionally 'I' has been preferred by purists but Partridge recommends the colloquial 'me', arguing that than is a preposition to be followed by the objective case – 'me'. Also, 'He is taller than I' sounds stilted:

> ... whether Grant Fox was a better kicker than he.
> (*Times*)

There is another option, 'He is taller than I am', where than is a conjunction followed by subject and verb, 'I am'. This has the advantage of being neither stilted nor colloquial. Prefer it in writing unless you're writing dialogue.

This formula becomes essential when 'than me' would be ambiguous. 'She likes him more than me' has the obvious meaning of 'She likes him more than she likes me.' So if you want to say 'She likes him more than I do', that is what you'd better say – as well as write.

thankfully *see* **sentence adverbs**

that

is often left out of sentences like 'He said that he would come'. Leaving that out saves space and makes the sentence less formal. But be careful when leaving that out may cause the reader to stumble:

He admitted the offence was serious.

He claimed the prize was not worth winning.

He learnt her name was Mary.

And there is ambiguity in:

She said before he arrived he should put on a tie.

Restoring that after she said or after arrived makes the sentence clear.

that, which

there is a continuing problem with 'that' and 'which'. According to traditional grammar, 'that' should be used in defining clauses:

This is the house that Jack built.

Whereas 'which' should be used in non-defining clauses:

They bought Fred's house, which was built in 1937.

'That Jack built' defines the house and doesn't have a comma before it; 'which was built in 1937' adds incidental information and should have a comma.

But many literate people – academics, novelists, journalists – do not always use 'that' for defining clauses. And the Queen, whose every utterance is carefully checked by her advisers, certainly doesn't. In her 2002 Christmas broadcast she said: 'All great religions have such times of renewal, moments to take stock before moving on to face the challenges *which* lie ahead.' And her royal website said: 'The Queen's Speech … outlines the legislation *which* the Government plans to introduce to Parliament in the coming session.'

In both cases, according to the rule, 'which' should be 'that'. So what's happening? Does the Queen no longer speak the Queen's English?

It makes more sense to say that the Queen's English has changed with (almost) everybody else's and become looser. It has long been accepted that 'who/whom' can be used instead of 'that' in defining clauses referring to people:

> This is the man who/that shot Liberty Valance.

In the same way 'that' can now be replaced by 'which' in defining clauses which don't refer to people without anybody (except pedants) even noticing.

But the position on non-defining clauses is different. If 'that' is used instead of 'which', it looks, sounds and is wrong:

> Michael Owen celebrates his 82nd-minute winner in Bratislava that gave England victory over Slovakia.
>
> (*Observer* picture caption)

'That' should be 'which'; for 'that' to work, 'his winner' would have to be changed to 'the winner'.

Then there is the problem of 'which and/but that', 'that and/but which' etc:

> You are a young crime writer with three books to your credit, which have all been reviewed well but that sold badly.
>
> (Miles Kington)

'That' is clearly wrong here. The change from 'which' to 'that' suggests that what follows is a different kind of clause – in fact it is the same. Change 'that' to 'which' or leave it out.

But what about William Carlos Williams' poem 'This is Just to Say'?

> I have eaten
> the plums
> that were in
> the icebox
> and which

you were probably
saving
for breakfast.
Forgive me
they were delicious
so sweet
and so cold.

Here 'that' is defining, 'which' non-defining; the change from one to
the other clarifies the meaning. The problem is the 'and' that connects
them, which in speech we would leave out. Williams had poetic
licence but in prose I think the 'and' is better left out.

theatregoer
is one word.

thespian
is facetious/pretentious for actor.

they, them, their *see* **he/she, h/she, he or she**

third world
no caps, but prefer developing countries.

though *see* **although, though**

till, until
but not til, 'til, 'till

time, at this moment in
use now.

titbit
not tidbit

titillate, titivate
to titillate is to excite, almost always sexually (titillating nude
drawings); to titivate is to smarten up.

toilet
once considered genteel, toilet is now the ordinary word – see **u/ non-u**.

ton, tonne, tun
a tonne is a metric ton and slightly heavier than a ton; a tun is a large cask for beer or wine.

Tonbridge, Kent
but Tunbridge Wells

top dollar
not top dollars, for high price

tornadoes
not tornados

torpedoes
not torpedos

torpid
sluggish, is confused with torrid, violently hot, as in this intended reference to passionate sex:

> 'torpid afternoons with her daughter's boyfriend'.
> *(Guardian)*

torrid *see* **torpid**

tortuous, torturous
tortuous, meaning winding, circuitous, is quite a common word; torturous, from torture, meaning causing torture, painful, is very rare. The words are easily confused, particularly by people who have never come across torturous: avoid using it unless you are sure your reader will understand you. Above all, don't use tortuous to refer to torture:

> Tully stayed home while Jack painted. But what she had thought would be fun turned out to be tortuous.
> (Paullina Simons)

trademark
but trade name

Trades Union Congress
but
trade union
plural trade unions

transatlantic
one word, no cap

transport
not transportation

troop
a troop is a body of soldiers, not an individual. Troops works as a general plural:

> Bring the troops home.

But this is confusing:

> The chief of the maquis ... did not know how many German troops he would be up against.
>
> (Adam Nossiter)

And this is ridiculous:

> ... concern about casualties – 55 troops have died since May 1.
>
> (*Christian Science Monitor*)

trousers *see* **pants**

trove
as in treasure trove, a find of valuable articles, has no plural.

truly
is misused in the same way as literally:

Like so many assassin's bullets, this was truly a shot heard around the world.

(Guardian)

See **rhetorical adverbs**.

try to
not try and. Try and (try and come to the party) is fine in informal speech but in writing try to is necessary.

tsar
not czar

T-shirt
not tee-shirt

Tunbridge Wells, Kent *see* **Tonbridge**

turkish delight
no caps

tyre
not tire for the tube round a wheel rim

U

u/non-u

these terms from the 1950s (for upper class and not upper class) are still in the dictionary but they are hardly ever used nowadays. This is because most of the original distinctions, eg scent (u)/perfume (non-u), wireless (u)/radio (non-u) and looking-glass (u)/mirror (non-u) no longer apply – if they ever did. In these cases the 'non-u' word is the generally accepted one. Toilet, which used to be non-u for lavatory, is now the ordinary word, used in public notices and other formal contexts (though it is not universally accepted); lavatory is now rare. The most common informal word is loo.

One or two distinctions, eg sorry (u)/ pardon (non-u), (table) napkin (u)/serviette (non-u) and sitting-room (u)/lounge (non-u), are still made by some people. Lady, traditionally non-u for woman, now seems to be generally accepted, except in books and television programmes for children, where woman is the more pc form.

ubiquitous

is a literary word for 'to be found everywhere'. It is an absolute adjective. You can't be more or less or quite or particularly or so ubiquitous: either you are everywhere or you're not. So the following are mistakes:

> Nesselrode pudding is particularly ubiquitous.
> (Nicola Humble)

> The urban fox is becoming bolder and more ubiquitous in London.
> (*Evening Standard*)

The most ubiquitous broadcaster in the country.
(*Australian*)

So widespread and ubiquitous is the tension around food that we almost take it for granted.
(Susie Orbach, *Guardian*)

The common word these writers needed was widespread – or common.

Ulster
the Irish province of Ulster consists of nine counties, six of them in Northern Ireland and three in the Republic. So it is a mistake to call Northern Ireland 'Ulster', though headline writers in British newspapers do so for their own convenience. This annoys Irish people.

unbiased
not unbiassed

unchristian
one word

underpants *see* pants

under the circumstances
should be *in* since the circumstances (from *circum*, Latin for around) are around not above you.

underway
is now one word (the ship is underway).

undoubtedly
not undoubtably

uninterested *see* disinterest, disinterested

union flag, jack
technically what is flown from public buildings and elsewhere on land is the union *flag* not the union jack. A jack is a small flag on a ship,

usually at the bow. This is a necessary distinction in certain contexts –
and essential knowledge for Trivial Pursuit and pub quizzes – but
'union jack' is universally understood to mean the flag.

unique

is an absolute adjective meaning the only one of its kind. You can't be
nearly or rather unique:

> It was an agreement ... nearly unique in the history of the
> European war/an initiative nearly unique in American
> diplomacy during the war.
>
> (Adam Nossiter)

> Two rather unique populist parties suddenly materialised as
> significant forces.
>
> (Joe Klein, *Guardian*)

'Two rather unique' is priceless.

unmistakable

not unmistakeable

up to a point, Lord Copper

this is one of those clichés based on allusion that most people get
wrong. In Evelyn Waugh's *Scoop* it is said in a toadying fashion by an
underling who disagrees with Lord Copper but is unable to say so – so
it actually means no. As with the curate's egg, misusing this cliché
parades ignorance rather than sophistication.

urban, urbane

urban means of or belonging to a city; urbane means refined and
courteous.

url

the address of a page on the web

us *see* I/me

use, utilise

use is the ordinary word for make use of (he used a saucepan for the tea, use your head, he used her for his own ends). There is no case for using utilise as a variation word in these contexts: it is merely pretentious:

> utilising the electric kettle and the little packets provided
> (Alice Thomas Ellis, quoted by Burchfield)

Some usage guides say that utilise has a special sense: put to use something that would otherwise be wasted (Trask); make use of something not intended for the job (Bryson). But in the examples they give, plain 'use' could easily be substituted for 'utilise' without meaning being lost. Partridge makes more sense on this: 'utilise, utilisation are, 99 times out of 100, much inferior to use, verb and noun; the one other time, they are merely inferior.'

utopian

no cap

u-turn

needs a hyphen.

v
not vs for versus (Spurs v Arsenal)

vaccination *see* **inoculation, vaccination**

variation
Fowler used the term 'elegant variation' for the habit of calling a spade a tool or a horticultural implement to avoid repeating the word spade. It was a fault, he said, committed by 'second-rate writers, those intent rather on expressing themselves prettily than on conveying their meaning clearly'. What he called the fatal influence was the advice given to young writers never to use the same word twice in a sentence.

It's as easy now as it was in Fowler's day (the 1920s) to find examples of this:

> IPC took her [Sly Bailey] on in 1989 and by 1994, aged 31, she was appointed to the board of the publishing company, becoming its youngest ever member. The Spurs fan continued to work her way up through the ranks.
>
> (*Guardian*)

This is from a profile of Sly Bailey in which there is no further mention of Spurs or football. 'Spurs fan' is variation for its own sake.

> Once again Wilhelm knocked on the kitchen door, but this time Doctor Stein was all smiles, and as bashful as a boy.
>
> (Doris Lessing)

Here 'Wilhelm' and 'Doctor Stein' are the same person; in Lessing's book *The Sweetest Dream*, after a few more Wilhelms there's even a third version – 'Wilhelm Stein'. Why not stick with Wilhelm and otherwise use 'he'?

> Part of Roseanne's behaviour can be explained by the comic's natural competitiveness.
>
> (John Lahr)

In this case too why not 'her' for 'the comic's'? Unless, of course, Lahr is saying something completely different and referring to the natural competitiveness of comics in general. But if Lahr does want to make this reference, it will be missed by most readers; as it stands the sentence is ambiguous.

This kind of variation (David Beckham ... the footballer, Zadie Smith ... the novelist, Brad Pitt ... the actor) is always irritating and occasionally confusing.

variety meat(s)
is an American euphemism for offal (heart, liver, kidney etc).

vatic
is literary for prophetic.

veld
not veldt

venal, venial
venal means able to be bought, corrupt (a venal official); venial means minor, excusable (a venial sin).

venetian blind
no caps

veranda
not verandah

verbal *see* **oral, verbal**

verbal noun *see* **gerund**

vest
as with pants there is the risk of confusion between British and American usage. This could be the American (over the shirt – waistcoat) rather than the British (under the shirt):

> Charles II decreed that vests would be the new court fashion for men.
>
> *(Sunday Times)*

virtually
is a rhetorical adverb used to mean almost:

> He [Tony Blair] said this was 'a highly exceptional, virtually unique case'.
>
> *(Guardian)*

See also: **rhetorical adverbs**.

virtuosos
is the plural of virtuoso.

virus *see* **bacterium, bug, microbe, virus**

vortexes
is the plural of vortex.

wagon
not waggon

wagons-lits
is the plural of wagon-lit, meaning sleeping-car.

waitress *see* **feminine forms**

waive, wave
to waive is to give up or refrain from taking (he waived his claim to the land); to wave is to move the hand in greeting.

waiver, waver
a waiver is the giving-up of a claim; to waver is to hesitate or falter.

walkie-talkie
not walky-talky for portable two-wave radio

Walkman
with cap, is a trade name; otherwise use personal stereo.

wash up
in Britain to wash up means to wash the dishes etc after a meal; in the US it usually means to wash your face and hands.

wastage, waste
wastage is loss resulting from use or natural causes (wastage of water caused by evaporation). Hence the term natural wastage, used of a reduction in an organisation's workforce caused by retirement and

resignation as opposed to dismissal. Waste, by contrast, implies criticism: a waste of water is the squandering of it.

wasteland

is one word but TS Eliot's poem is *The Waste Land*.

watershed

this is the line separating two river basins and so a dividing line or crucial point (the second Iraq war was a watershed for New Labour). Watershed should not be used to mean a drainage or catchment area.

we *see* I/me

weather conditions

conditions is a pointless addition to weather (they had bad weather conditions on holiday).

weave

this is two words in one. To weave (cloth) becomes wove, woven in the past (he wove a pattern in the shirt); to weave meaning to move to and fro, wind in and out, becomes weaved (he weaved his way through the traffic).

web, the

no cap

website

not web-site, web site

weirdos

not weirdoes

Welch

is an old form of Welsh. It survives in the Royal Welch Fusiliers (but not the Welsh Guards).

wellnigh

is literary for very nearly.

welsh

to welsh means to fail to keep a promise or honour an obligation (he welshed on the deal). Burchfield stresses that the word may not have anything to do with the Welsh people. But using it risks offending those Welsh people who are not language scholars.

welsh rabbit, rarebit

use rabbit which was the original term for melted cheese on toast. Rarebit makes no sense since cheese on toast is hardly an exotic delicacy and it is not undercooked. The origin of the name welsh rabbit is obscure: it may or may not be a snide English joke at the expense of the Welsh (on the grounds that they were too poor to eat meat).

what

can be a problem at the beginning of a sentence. Should it be 'What I like *is* holidays abroad' or 'What I like *are* holidays abroad'? The experts disagree. Fowler and Partridge insist on the singular while Gowers and the Longman guide say that the plural is permissible. In his revision of Fowler Burchfield hedges his bets, calling Fowler 'unusually dogmatic' but concluding: 'For the sake of simplicity it is better to adhere to (his) rule than to make it subject to qualification.'

It may be possible to convert the whole sentence into the singular:

What I like is a holiday abroad.

Alternatively, in writing you can forget the conversational rhetoric and use the plain 'I like holidays abroad.'

whence

is literary for from what place. From whence, which is used in the King James bible, is archaic: the from is clearly redundant.

wherefore

does not mean where but why ('Wherefore art thou Romeo?').

wherever

not whereever

whet

not wet the appetite

which *see* **that, which**

while

not whilst, which is literary. Be careful when using while to mean and, although, on the other hand, since its primary meaning is at the same time as:

> The head gave a short speech of welcome while her deputy announced the results.

'And' would be better here.

whisky, whiskey

whisky is scotch and Canadian; whiskey is Irish and American.

whither

is archaic for to what place.

whizz-kid

not whiz-kid

who, whom

in traditional grammar who is subjective (who is your guest?) and whom is objective (whom did you invite?/to whom did you send an invitation?). But in speech and increasingly in writing who is replacing whom. The following are becoming standard:

> Who did you invite?

> Who did you send an invitation to?

Whom is still used after a preposition (to whom it may concern).
  Some people, struggling to be correct, put whom where who is needed:

The black woman, whom he knew was Rebecca, now served the lunch.

(Doris Lessing)

But there is a similar construction which does take whom:

The black woman, whom he knew to be Rebecca, now served the lunch.

whodunit
not whodunnit

whoever, whomever
if whom is dying, whomever is dead: use whoever whenever.

whys and wherefores *see* **repetition**

wick *see* **rhyming slang**

wicketkeeper
is one word.

wireless *see* **u/non-u**

-wise
is a trendy suffix wordswise. Don't use it in formal writing except in accepted cases like likewise and clockwise.

wisteria
not wistaria for the plant

with
does not mean and. Tea with milk means tea with milk added and 'He goes to school with his friend' is grammatically identical with 'He goes to school with his satchel.' Putting the 'with' first doesn't change anything.

Best known for his novel *Charlotte's Web*, the essayist EB

White was frustrated by an early job in publicity and so, with a Cornell friend, Howard Cushman, they set off through the West.

Correct the sentence by deleting they.

within

has two uses distinct from in. It is used in phrases like 'within reach' and 'delivery within five days'. And it is a literary alternative to inside:

The cathedral stands within the city walls.

It should not be used as a longwinded way of saying in:

Within Zimbabwe itself ... I find only two Mugabe supporters.

(Alexander Fuller)

Her meteoric success has caused bitter jealousies within literary London.

(*Guardian* leader on Zadie Smith)

The weapon was kept within Mr Packer's office.

(*Australian*)

wits' end

has the apostrophe after the s.

Women's Lib

don't use this archaic short form – unless you want to belittle the women's movement.

wondrous

is literary/archaic.

World Trade Centre
not Center

world war
first/second world war, no caps, not World War I/II, One/Two

worldwide
but

world wide web, www
in urls

worthwhile
is one word (his visit was worthwhile) but note: it was worth his while.

wrack
is seaweed; see **rack**.

wunderkind
no cap or italic, for child prodigy or precocious youth; the plural is
wunderkinder.

X

Xerox
is a trade name so use photocopy.

Xmas
the common short form for Christmas, upsets some people, who consider it vulgar, commercial etc. In fact the X represents the first letter (chi) of the Greek word for Christ.

x-ray
not X-ray

yang *see* **yin**

Yankee, Yank
were once common British nicknames for Americans. In the US a Yankee was originally a New Englander, then a Northerner in the Civil War.

year
use plain 'in 2000' not 'in the year 2000'.

year's/years' time
adding the word 'time' to expressions like 'in a year' and 'in two years' is padding: 'Come back in two years' not 'in two years' time'.

yeses
not yesses

yin
yin and yang are the two basic principles of Chinese philosophy.

yogurt
not yoghurt, yoghourt, yaourt

yoke, yolk
yoke (for oxen) is confused with yolk (of egg).

yonder
is archaic for over there (I espy yonder castle); it does not mean past:

> In yonder years my head would have crowned Traitors' Gate
> for suggesting that the king's 'companion' be made queen.
> (Guardian)

yorkshire pudding, terrier
no need for caps

you and I *see* **I/me**

yours
not your's for the possessive

yo–yo
not yoyo

Z

zeitgeist
spirit of the age, does not need caps or italics.

zeros
is the plural of zero.

zigzag
not zig-zag

zip code
the US postcode, doesn't need a cap.

zombie
not zomby for revived corpse

zucchini
the Italian plural, is often used in the US and Australia for courgettes (baby marrow).

FURTHER READING

Amis, Kingsley, *The King's English*, HarperCollins, 1997

Amis, Martin, *The War Against Cliché*, Vintage, 2002

Bickerton, Anthea, *American English/English American: A Two-Way Glossary of Words in Daily Use on Both Sides of the Atlantic*, Abson Books, 1985

—— *Australian English/English Australian* (second edition), Abson Books, 1988

Bryson, Bill, *Troublesome Words* (third edition), Viking, 2001

Burchfield, RW (ed), *The New Fowler's Modern English Usage* (third edition), OUP, 1996

Burridge, Kate, *Blooming English*, ABC Books for the Australian Broadcasting Corporation, 2002

Cameron, Deborah, *Verbal Hygiene*, Routledge, 1995

The Chambers Dictionary, Chambers, 1998

Cochrane, James, *Between You and I*, Icon Books, 2003

Crystal, David, *The Cambridge Encyclopedia of the English Language*, CUP, 1995

—— *The Economist Style Guide* (sixth edition), Profile Books, 2000

Fowler, HW, *A Dictionary of Modern English Usage*, original 1926 edition, republished by Omega Books, 1984

Goodman, Neville and Edwards, Martin, *Medical Writing* (second edition), CUP, 1997

Gowers, Sir Ernest, *The Complete Plain Words* (second edition), revised by Sir Bruce Fraser, HM Stationery Office and Pelican Books, 1973

Greenbaum, Sidney, and Whitcut, Janet, *Longman Guide to English Usage*, Longman, 1988

Jespersen, Otto, *Essentials of English Grammar*, Allen & Unwin, 1933

Mayes, Ian, *Corrections and Clarifications*, Guardian Newspapers, 2000

Mayes, Ian, *More Corrections and Clarifications*, Guardian Newspapers, 2002

Moss, Norman, *The Hutchinson British–American Dictionary* (third edition), Helicon, 1994

Partridge, Eric, *Usage and Abusage* (third edition), revised by Janet Whitcut, Penguin Books, 1999

Pinker, Steven, *The Language Instinct*, Penguin Books, 1995

Ritter, RM (ed and comp), *The Oxford Dictionary for Writers and Editors* (*ODWE*) (second edition), 2000

Room, Adrian, *Brewer's Dictionary of Phrase and Fable*, (16th edn) Cassell, 1999

Strunk, William, *The Elements of Style* (third edition), revised by EB White, Macmillan (New York), 1979

Trask, RL, *Mind the Gaffe*, Penguin Books, 2001
Truss, Lynne, *Eats, Shoots & Leaves*, Profile Books, 2003
Wardhaugh, Ronald, *Proper English*, Blackwell, 1999
Waterhouse, Keith, *English Our English*, Viking, 1991